MAKE THIS YEAR YOUR BEST YEAR

PODCAST

Your Way to Success

M L Ruscsak

CHAPTER 1: WHAT IS PODCASTING?

❖ Definition of podcasting
❖ How podcasting differs from traditional radio and other forms of media
❖ Popular types of podcasts
❖ Examples of successful podcasts

What is Podcasting?

In the digital age, podcasting has emerged as a popular medium for sharing audio content over the internet. But what exactly is podcasting, and how does it work?

At its core, podcasting is a way to distribute audio content over the internet. It's similar to radio broadcasting, but with a few key differences. Whereas radio shows are broadcast live and listened to in real-time, podcasts are pre-recorded and then uploaded to the internet for listeners to download and listen to at their convenience. Podcasts can be listened to on a variety of devices, including smartphones, tablets, and computers.

Podcasts come in a wide range of formats and genres, from news and politics to sports, comedy, and true crime. Some podcasts are hosted by individuals or small teams, while others are produced by large media companies. Many podcasts are produced on a regular schedule, with new episodes released weekly or monthly.

One of the key features of podcasting is its ability to reach a niche audience. Because podcasts are pre-recorded and can be accessed from anywhere with an internet connection, listeners can find shows that cater to their specific interests, no matter how obscure. This makes podcasting a powerful tool for building a loyal audience and connecting with listeners who are passionate about the same topics as you.

Podcasting has exploded in popularity over the past decade, with millions of people around the world listening to podcasts on a regular basis. The rise of smartphones and other mobile devices has made it easier than ever to access podcasts on-the-go, whether you're commuting to work or going for a jog. With so many podcasts available, it can be difficult to keep up with all the latest shows and trends, but the growing popularity of podcasting shows no signs of slowing down anytime soon.

In summary, podcasting is a powerful medium for distributing audio content over the internet. It allows producers to connect with a niche audience, build a loyal following, and share their message with the world. Whether you're a hobbyist, a professional broadcaster, or a business owner looking to reach a wider audience, podcasting offers a unique and effective way to connect with listeners and share your message.

How Podcasting Differs from Traditional Radio and Other Forms of Media

While podcasting and traditional radio share many similarities, there are also some key differences that set the two mediums apart. Understanding these differences can help you create better content and reach a wider audience.

Here are some of the ways in which podcasting differs from traditional radio and other forms of media:

On-demand listening: One of the biggest differences between podcasting and traditional radio is the ability to listen on-demand. Unlike traditional radio, which is broadcast live, podcasts can be downloaded and listened to at any time. This means that listeners can access your content whenever it's convenient for them, whether they're on a commute or working out at the gym.

Niche audiences: Podcasts are often created for specific niche audiences, allowing producers to target their content to a specific group of listeners. This is in contrast to traditional radio, which often has a broader audience. This means that podcasters can create content that is highly specific to their listeners' interests, resulting in a more engaged and loyal audience.

Lower barrier to entry: Traditional radio broadcasting typically requires a lot of expensive equipment and infrastructure. Podcasting, on the other hand, has a much lower barrier to entry. All you need to get started is a microphone, a computer, and an internet connection. This means that anyone can create a podcast and share their voice with the world.

Longer format: Another key difference between podcasting and traditional radio is the length of the content. While traditional radio segments are often short and interspersed with commercials, podcasts can run for hours at a time. This allows podcasters to dive deeper into a topic and create a more immersive listening experience.

More creative control: Because podcasting is a relatively new medium, there are few rules and regulations governing its content. This gives podcasters more creative control over their content, allowing them to experiment with different formats and styles. This freedom can result in more interesting and engaging content that is tailored to a specific audience.

Global reach: Unlike traditional radio, which is often limited to a local or regional audience, podcasts can reach a global audience. This is because podcasts can be accessed from anywhere in the world with an internet connection. This means that podcasters can reach a wider audience and build a global following.

In summary, podcasting differs from traditional radio and other forms of media in several key ways. Podcasts offer on-demand listening, target niche audiences, have a lower barrier to entry, can run for longer periods of time, give more creative control to the producers, and have a global reach. Understanding these differences can help you create better content and reach a wider audience through podcasting.

Popular Types of Podcasts

Podcasts have become an increasingly popular form of media, with millions of listeners tuning in to their favorite shows every day. From true crime to comedy, there's a podcast out there for everyone. Here are some of the most popular types of podcasts:

True Crime: True crime podcasts are some of the most popular podcasts out there. These podcasts explore real-life crimes and mysteries, often with a focus on unsolved cases. True crime podcasts often feature in-depth interviews with law enforcement officials, crime scene investigators, and even the victims themselves.

Comedy: Comedy podcasts are another popular genre. These podcasts often feature comedians discussing a wide range of topics, from pop culture to politics. Some of the most popular comedy podcasts include The Joe Rogan Experience and My Favorite Murder.

News and Politics: News and politics podcasts are a great way to stay informed on current events. These podcasts cover everything from local news to international politics, often with a focus on in-depth analysis and expert commentary. Some of the most popular news and politics podcasts include The Daily and Pod Save America.

Sports: Sports podcasts are a great way for fans to stay up-to-date on their favorite teams and players. These podcasts cover a wide range of sports, from football to soccer. Some of the most popular sports podcasts include Pardon My Take and The Bill Simmons Podcast.

Business and Finance: Business and finance podcasts are a great way to learn about the world of finance and entrepreneurship. These podcasts often feature interviews with successful business leaders and experts, and cover topics such as investing, entrepreneurship, and career development. Some of the most popular business and finance podcasts include The Tim Ferriss Show and How I Built This.

Pop Culture: Pop culture podcasts are a great way to stay up-to-date on the latest trends in entertainment. These podcasts cover everything from movies and TV shows to music and fashion. Some of the most popular pop culture podcasts include Pop Culture Happy Hour and The Rewatchables.

Personal Development: Personal development podcasts are a great way to improve your personal and professional life. These podcasts cover a wide range of topics, from mindfulness and meditation to productivity and goal setting. Some of the most popular personal development podcasts include The School of Greatness and Optimal Living Daily.

In summary, there are many different types of podcasts to choose from, and each one offers a unique listening experience. Whether you're interested in true crime, comedy, news and politics, sports, business and finance, pop culture, or personal development, there's a podcast out there for you. By exploring different types of podcasts, you can discover new perspectives and gain valuable insights into a wide range of topics.

Examples of Successful Podcasts

Podcasts have become increasingly popular in recent years, with millions of listeners tuning in to their favorite shows every day. Some podcasts have become hugely successful, with large audiences and dedicated followings. Here are some examples of successful podcasts:

The Joe Rogan Experience: Hosted by comedian and MMA commentator Joe Rogan, The Joe Rogan Experience is one of the most popular podcasts out there. The show features long-form interviews with a wide range of guests, from comedians to scientists to politicians. The show has become known for its free-wheeling conversations and unfiltered discussions.

Serial: Serial is a true crime podcast that became a cultural phenomenon when it first launched in 2014. The first season of the show focused on the case of Adnan Syed, who was convicted of murdering his ex-girlfriend. The show's in-depth reporting and storytelling captivated audiences, and it quickly became one of the most popular podcasts of all time.

Radiolab: Radiolab is a science and storytelling podcast that explores a wide range of topics, from biology to physics to philosophy. The show's hosts, Jad Abumrad and Robert Krulwich, use a mix of interviews, sound effects, and music to create a unique and immersive listening experience. Radiolab has won numerous awards, including a Peabody Award and a National Science Foundation grant.

Stuff You Should Know: Stuff You Should Know is an educational podcast that covers a wide range of topics, from history to science to pop culture. The show's hosts, Josh Clark and Chuck Bryant, use a conversational style to explain complex topics in a way that's easy to understand. The show has a large and dedicated following, with millions of downloads every month.

How I Built This: How I Built This is a business and entrepreneurship podcast that features interviews with successful entrepreneurs and business leaders. The show's host, Guy Raz, explores the stories behind some of the world's most successful companies, from Airbnb to Spanx. The show has become known for its inspiring and insightful interviews, and it has won numerous awards, including a Webby Award and a Gracie Award.

My Favorite Murder: My Favorite Murder is a true crime and comedy podcast hosted by comedians Karen Kilgariff and Georgia Hardstark. The show explores a wide range of true crime cases, from well-known cases like the Golden State Killer to lesser-known cases like the Toy Box Killer. The show's hosts use humor to explore some of the darkest aspects of human nature, and the show has become hugely popular, with a dedicated fan base known as the "murderinos."

TED Radio Hour: TED Radio Hour is a podcast that features highlights from some of the most popular TED Talks. Each episode focuses on a different theme, from creativity to the human brain to artificial intelligence. The show's host, Guy Raz, interviews the speakers and explores the ideas behind their talks. The show has become known for its inspiring and thought-provoking content, and it has won numerous awards, including a Webby Award and a Peabody Award.

In summary, there are many successful podcasts out there, with a wide range of topics and styles. These podcasts have attracted large audiences and dedicated followings, and they demonstrate the power of the medium to engage and entertain listeners. By studying successful podcasts, you can gain valuable insights into what makes a podcast work and how to create a show that resonates with listeners.

CHAPTER 2: HISTORY OF PODCASTING

- ❖ Early history of podcasting
- ❖ Key players and pioneers in the podcasting world
- ❖ Milestones in the development of podcasting technology and distribution
- ❖ How podcasting has evolved over time

Early history of podcasting

The history of podcasting is a fascinating story that highlights the innovative spirit of humanity. It all started in the early 2000s, when a few tech-savvy individuals began experimenting with new ways to distribute and consume digital media.

The term "podcasting" is a combination of "iPod," Apple's popular portable media player at the time, and "broadcasting," which refers to the traditional method of distributing audio content over the airwaves. Despite its name, podcasting is not limited to the iPod or any other device, and can be consumed on a wide range of devices.

The origins of podcasting can be traced back to the early days of blogging. In 2000, Dave Winer, a software developer and blogger, created an application called "Radio UserLand" that allowed users to create and distribute audio content using RSS feeds. This was the first step towards creating a platform for podcasting.

In 2003, Adam Curry, a former MTV VJ and technology enthusiast, began experimenting with Winer's software and started recording and distributing his own radio show online. Curry coined the term "podcasting" to describe this new form of online broadcasting, and the name quickly caught on.

Around the same time, other pioneers of podcasting were also emerging, including Christopher Lydon, who launched the "Open Source" podcast, and Ben Hammersley, who wrote an article for The Guardian about the emerging trend. These early adopters helped to popularize podcasting and demonstrate its potential as a new form of media.

One of the earliest and most popular podcasts was "The Ricky Gervais Show," which debuted in 2005 and quickly gained a massive following. The show featured British comedian Ricky Gervais and his friends, Stephen Merchant and Karl Pilkington, discussing a wide range of topics in a humorous and irreverent style. The success of this podcast helped to cement podcasting as a legitimate form of entertainment and paved the way for future podcasters to follow.

Since then, the popularity of podcasting has continued to grow at a rapid pace, with a wide range of shows covering everything from news and politics to comedy and true crime. Today, there are over 2 million active podcasts available, with new shows launching every day.

In conclusion, the early history of podcasting is a testament to the power of innovation and creativity. From humble beginnings as an experiment in online broadcasting, podcasting has evolved into a mainstream form of media with a vast and diverse audience. As the technology continues to improve and new voices enter the podcasting landscape, the future of this exciting medium looks brighter than ever.

Key players and pioneers in the podcasting world

The world of podcasting is home to a wide range of creators, hosts, and producers, many of whom have played a pivotal role in shaping the industry. From early pioneers who paved the way for the medium's success to current leaders who continue to innovate and push the boundaries of podcasting, these key players have left an indelible mark on the podcasting landscape.

One of the earliest and most influential figures in podcasting is Adam Curry, often referred to as the "Podfather." In addition to coining the term "podcasting," Curry was instrumental in developing and promoting RSS feeds as a way to distribute audio content. He is also the co-host of "No Agenda," a popular news and commentary podcast that has been running for over a decade.

Another key player in the podcasting world is Marc Maron, the host of "WTF with Marc Maron." Maron's podcast, which began in 2009, features interviews with a wide range of celebrities and notable figures, and has been credited with helping to popularize the interview format in podcasting. Maron's success also paved the way for other comedians and entertainers to launch their own podcasts.

Ira Glass, the host and producer of "This American Life," is another major figure in the world of podcasting. Glass and his team have been producing the award-winning radio show since 1995, and in 2006 they began releasing the show as a podcast. "This American Life" helped to establish the narrative storytelling format that has since become a hallmark of many popular podcasts.

Serial, a true crime podcast produced by This American Life, became a cultural phenomenon when it was released in 2014. The podcast's deep dive into the 1999 murder of high school student Hae Min Lee and the subsequent conviction of her ex-boyfriend Adnan Syed captivated millions of listeners and helped to propel podcasting into the mainstream. The show's host, Sarah Koenig, is widely regarded as one of the most influential figures in podcasting.

Other key players in the podcasting world include Jad Abumrad and Robert Krulwich, the hosts of the science and culture podcast "Radiolab"; Roman Mars, the host of the design and architecture podcast "99% Invisible"; and Joe Rogan, the host of the popular interview podcast "The Joe Rogan Experience."

In conclusion, the world of podcasting is home to a diverse and talented group of creators and innovators, many of whom have played a pivotal role in shaping the industry. Whether they are early pioneers who paved the way for podcasting's success or current leaders who continue to push the boundaries of the medium, these key players have left an indelible mark on podcasting, and their contributions will be felt for years to come.

Milestones in the development of podcasting technology and distribution

Podcasting has come a long way since its inception, with numerous technological advancements and distribution platforms that have enabled the medium to grow and flourish. Here are some of the most significant milestones in the development of podcasting technology and distribution.

The birth of podcasting can be traced back to the early 2000s, when RSS feeds were used to distribute audio content. In 2003, Dave Winer, one of the pioneers of RSS technology, created a tool called "Enclosure," which enabled audio files to be included in RSS feeds. This development paved the way for the creation of the first podcasts.

One of the key milestones in the development of podcasting technology was the release of Apple's iTunes 4.9 in 2005, which included support for podcasts. This made it easy for users to discover and subscribe to podcasts, and provided a platform for podcasters to distribute their shows to a wider audience.

In 2006, podcasting received a major boost when NPR's "This American Life" began distributing its show as a podcast. The show's popularity helped to establish podcasting as a legitimate medium for storytelling and news, and paved the way for other radio shows to do the same.

Another significant development in the world of podcasting was the introduction of smartphones and mobile devices. As more people began using their phones as their primary device for consuming media, podcasters had to adapt to the changing landscape. In 2012, Apple introduced a standalone Podcasts app for iOS, making it even easier for users to discover and subscribe to podcasts on their mobile devices.

In recent years, new technologies such as smart speakers and voice assistants have further expanded the reach of podcasting. With devices like Amazon Echo and Google Home, users can listen to podcasts hands-free and with minimal effort. This has made podcasts more accessible than ever before.

As podcasting has grown in popularity, so too have the distribution platforms. While Apple remains the dominant player in podcasting, other platforms such as Spotify, Google Podcasts, and Stitcher have also emerged as major players in the industry. These platforms offer podcasters new opportunities to reach new audiences and monetize their shows.

In conclusion, the development of podcasting technology and distribution has been a constant process of innovation and evolution. From the early days of RSS feeds and Enclosure, to the rise of mobile devices and voice assistants, podcasting has adapted and grown alongside new technologies. As podcasting continues to gain popularity, we can expect even more innovations and developments in the years to come.

How podcasting has evolved over time

Podcasting has come a long way since its humble beginnings in the early 2000s. Over the years, it has evolved in numerous ways, from the technology used to create and distribute podcasts, to the types of content that are produced. Here are some of the key ways that podcasting has evolved over time.

One of the most significant changes in the world of podcasting has been the sheer number of shows that are now available. When podcasting first began, there were only a handful of shows available, most of which were produced by hobbyists and enthusiasts. Today, there are millions of podcasts available on a wide range of topics, from true crime to comedy to business and beyond.

Another major development in the world of podcasting has been the rise of professional content. While many podcasts are still produced by amateurs and hobbyists, there are now more professional studios and production companies getting involved in the industry. This has led to an increase in the quality of the production values and a wider range of formats and genres available.

The way that podcasts are consumed has also changed significantly over time. When podcasting first began, most people listened to shows on their desktop computers or laptops. However, with the rise of smartphones and mobile devices, the majority of podcast consumption now happens on mobile devices. This has led to changes in the way that podcasts are produced, with many shows now being optimized for listening on mobile devices.

Another significant development in the world of podcasting has been the rise of monetization. While podcasting began as a hobbyist pursuit, more and more creators are now looking to monetize their shows. This has led to the rise of advertising, sponsorship, and other forms of revenue generation. It has also led to the creation of more professional networks and studios that offer resources and support to podcasters looking to monetize their shows.

Finally, podcasting has become more integrated into the mainstream media landscape. While podcasting was once considered a niche medium, it is now considered a legitimate form of media. This has led to more cross-over between traditional media and podcasting, with many podcasts being produced by established media companies, and more traditional media outlets launching their own podcasting initiatives.

In conclusion, podcasting has evolved significantly over time. From its early days as a hobbyist pursuit to its current status as a legitimate form of media, podcasting has undergone many changes and developments. As technology and media continue to evolve, we can expect podcasting to continue to adapt and change in new and exciting ways.

CHAPTER 3: BENEFITS OF PODCASTING

❖ Why podcasting is a valuable form of communication and entertainment

❖ Advantages of podcasting over other types of media

❖ How podcasting can help businesses and individuals reach new audiences

❖ Examples of successful podcasters and their success stories

Why podcasting is a valuable form of communication and entertainment

Podcasting has become an increasingly popular form of communication and entertainment in recent years, with millions of people tuning in to listen to their favorite shows every day. But what makes podcasting such a valuable form of media? Here are some of the key reasons why podcasting is so popular and valuable.

First and foremost, podcasting offers a level of convenience that is unmatched by other forms of media. Because podcasts can be downloaded and listened to on-demand, listeners can enjoy their favorite shows at any time, whether they are on a long commute, working out at the gym, or just relaxing at home. This level of convenience has made podcasting an incredibly popular way for people to consume media.

Another key advantage of podcasting is the depth and breadth of content available. Unlike traditional radio or television, which are often limited to a specific format or genre, podcasts cover a wide range of topics and interests. From news and current events to true crime, comedy, and business, there is a podcast for almost every interest and passion. This level of variety and diversity makes podcasting an incredibly valuable form of media.

Podcasting also offers a unique level of intimacy and connection between creators and listeners. Because podcasts are often hosted by individuals or small groups of people, listeners can feel a personal connection with the hosts and guests. This personal connection can help build loyalty and trust between listeners and creators, which is a valuable asset in today's media landscape.

Another key advantage of podcasting is the level of engagement and interaction it offers. Many podcasts feature lively discussions, interviews with guests, and opportunities for listener feedback and participation. This level of engagement can help build a sense of community around a podcast, which is incredibly valuable for both creators and listeners.

Finally, podcasting offers a level of authenticity and credibility that is hard to find in other forms of media. Because podcasts are often produced independently or by smaller studios, they are often free from the constraints and biases of larger media organizations. This independence and authenticity can help build trust and credibility with listeners, which is a valuable asset in today's media landscape.

In conclusion, podcasting is a valuable form of communication and entertainment for a variety of reasons. Its convenience, variety, intimacy, engagement, and authenticity make it an incredibly popular and valuable form of media. As the world of media continues to evolve, podcasting is sure to remain an important and influential part of the media landscape.

Advantages of podcasting over other types of media

Podcasting has quickly become one of the most popular and valuable forms of media in the world. While other forms of media, such as radio, television, and print, still have their place, there are several key advantages that podcasting offers over these other types of media.

One of the biggest advantages of podcasting is its convenience. Unlike traditional media, which often requires viewers or listeners to tune in at a specific time or place, podcasts can be downloaded and listened to at any time, on any device. This means that listeners can enjoy their favorite podcasts while on the go, whether they're commuting, working out, or just relaxing at home.

Another advantage of podcasting is its flexibility and accessibility. Because podcasts are typically produced independently or by smaller studios, they are often free from the constraints of larger media organizations. This means that podcasts can cover a wide range of topics and interests, and can be produced in a variety of formats and styles. This level of flexibility and accessibility is a key advantage over other types of media, which may be more limited in their scope and reach.

Podcasting also offers a unique level of engagement and interaction with listeners. Many podcasts feature lively discussions, interviews with guests, and opportunities for listener feedback and participation. This level of engagement can help build a sense of community around a podcast, which is incredibly valuable for both creators and listeners. It can also help build a loyal and dedicated audience, which is a key asset for any media platform.

Another advantage of podcasting is its low barrier to entry. Unlike traditional media, which often requires a significant amount of resources and funding to produce, podcasting can be done with relatively simple equipment and a small team. This means that anyone with an idea and a microphone can create their own podcast and share their voice with the world.

Finally, podcasting offers a level of authenticity and credibility that is hard to find in other forms of media. Because podcasts are often produced independently or by smaller studios, they are often free from the biases and constraints of larger media organizations. This independence and authenticity can help build trust and credibility with listeners, which is a valuable asset in today's media landscape.

In conclusion, podcasting offers several key advantages over other types of media, including its convenience, flexibility, engagement, accessibility, low barrier to entry, and authenticity. As the world of media continues to evolve, podcasting is sure to remain an important and influential part of the media landscape.

How podcasting can help businesses and individuals reach new audiences

Podcasting has become an increasingly popular way for businesses and individuals to reach new audiences, share knowledge and expertise, and connect with people all over the world. Here are some ways in which podcasting can help you expand your reach:

Podcasting is an easily accessible medium: Podcasts can be downloaded and listened to on a variety of devices, including smartphones, tablets, and computers. This means that listeners can tune in from anywhere at any time, making it a convenient and accessible medium for reaching new audiences.

Podcasts allow for long-form content: Unlike other forms of content, such as blog posts or social media updates, podcasts allow for longer-form content. This means that you can dive deeper into a topic, explore multiple angles, and provide more comprehensive information to your audience.

Podcasts build trust and credibility: By consistently sharing your knowledge and expertise on a particular topic, you can establish yourself as a thought leader in your industry. Over time, this can help you build trust and credibility with your audience, which can translate into new business opportunities, partnerships, and collaborations.

Podcasts foster a sense of community: Podcasts can help you connect with your listeners in a more personal and intimate way. By sharing your voice and personality, you can create a sense of community and belonging that can help you build a loyal and engaged audience.

Podcasts can be repurposed: The content you create for your podcast can be repurposed for other forms of content, such as blog posts, social media updates, or even videos. This allows you to get more mileage out of your content, while also reaching different audiences on different platforms.

Overall, podcasting can be an incredibly valuable tool for businesses and individuals who are looking to reach new audiences, share their expertise, and build trust and credibility in their industry. By consistently producing high-quality content that resonates with your target audience, you can establish yourself as a thought leader and build a loyal following that can help you achieve your goals.

Examples of successful podcasters and their success stories

Rachel Hollis: Rachel Hollis is the host of the "Rise" podcast, which focuses on personal development and empowerment. She is also the author of several bestselling self-help books, including "Girl, Wash Your Face" and "Girl, Stop Apologizing." Through her podcast and books, Hollis has built a community of millions of women who are inspired by her message of self-love, confidence, and resilience.

Alex Blumberg: Alex Blumberg is the founder of Gimlet Media, a podcasting company that produces several successful podcasts, including "Startup" and "Reply All." Blumberg is a former radio producer who has won numerous awards for his work in public radio. In 2014, he decided to start his own podcasting company, which has since grown into one of the most successful podcast networks in the world.

Jay Shetty: Jay Shetty is a former monk who hosts the "On Purpose" podcast, which focuses on personal growth, spirituality, and mindfulness. He has interviewed a variety of guests, including Deepak Chopra, Kobe Bryant, and Alicia Keys, and has built a massive following of listeners who are inspired by his positive message.

Jad Abumrad and Robert Krulwich: Jad Abumrad and Robert Krulwich are the hosts of the "Radiolab" podcast, which explores a variety of scientific and philosophical topics in a creative and engaging way. The show has won numerous awards, including a Peabody Award and a National Academies Communication Award, and has been praised for its innovative storytelling and production.

Aminatou Sow and Ann Friedman: Aminatou Sow and Ann Friedman are the hosts of the "Call Your Girlfriend" podcast, which focuses on politics, culture, and current events from a feminist perspective. The show has been praised for its engaging and humorous tone, and has built a loyal following of listeners who appreciate its smart and insightful commentary.

Each of these podcasters has achieved success in their own unique way, but they all share a common thread: a passion for their topics and a commitment to producing high-quality, engaging content. By building a loyal following of listeners who are inspired by their message, they have been able to achieve both personal and professional success in the world of podcasting.

CHAPTER 4: UNDERSTANDING THE PODCASTING LANDSCAPE

- ❖ Overview of the current podcasting landscape
- ❖ Key trends and developments in the industry
- ❖ Major players in the podcasting world, including platforms, hosting services, and networks
- ❖ Challenges and opportunities in the podcasting industry

Overview of the current podcasting landscape

Podcasting has come a long way since its inception in the early 2000s. Today, podcasting has become an incredibly popular medium, with an estimated 100 million Americans listening to at least one podcast per month. In this chapter, we will explore the current podcasting landscape, including trends, listener demographics, and popular genres.

Podcasting Trends

Podcasting is growing at a rapid pace. According to a recent survey, 55% of Americans have listened to a podcast, up from 51% in 2019. This increase in podcast listening is due in part to the rise of smartphones, which have made it easier for people to access podcasts on-the-go. In addition, the COVID-19 pandemic has led to an increase in podcast listening, as people spend more time at home and seek new forms of entertainment.

Listener Demographics

Podcasting is a medium that appeals to a wide range of listeners. According to the same survey, the average podcast listener is 39 years old, and 51% are male. In terms of education, 45% of podcast listeners have a college degree or higher. Additionally, podcast listeners tend to have higher incomes, with 41% of listeners earning over $75,000 per year.

Popular Genres

There are countless genres of podcasts, each with its own unique appeal. Some of the most popular genres include:

True Crime: True crime podcasts have exploded in popularity in recent years, with shows like Serial and My Favorite Murder captivating audiences.

News and Politics: Podcasts have become an important source of news and political commentary. Shows like The Daily from The New York Times and Pod Save America have become go-to sources for news and analysis.

Comedy: Podcasts have also become a hub for comedy, with shows like The Joe Rogan Experience and My Brother, My Brother and Me providing endless laughs.

Business and Entrepreneurship: Podcasts have become an invaluable resource for business owners and entrepreneurs. Shows like How I Built This and The Tim Ferriss Show offer insights into the business world and tips for success.

Personal Development: Podcasts focused on personal development have also gained a large following. Shows like The School of Greatness and The Tony Robbins Podcast provide listeners with inspiration and advice for self-improvement.

Conclusion

The current podcasting landscape is diverse and growing, with new shows and genres being added all the time. Whether you're looking for true crime, news and politics, comedy, business insights, or personal development, there is a podcast out there for everyone. With the rise of smartphones and the convenience of on-demand listening, it's no surprise that podcasting has become one of the most popular forms of entertainment and communication in the modern era.

Key trends and developments in the industry

Podcasting has become an increasingly popular form of media over the last decade, with new shows being created and distributed every day. As the industry continues to grow, there are several key trends and developments that are shaping the podcasting landscape.

Growth in listenership: According to a report by Edison Research, the number of Americans who have ever listened to a podcast reached 78% in 2021, up from 44% in 2018. This growth is due in part to the increased availability of podcasts on a wide range of topics, as well as the convenience of listening on-demand.

Expansion of podcast genres: In the early days of podcasting, shows tended to focus on news, politics, and technology. However, as the medium has evolved, new genres have emerged, including true crime, comedy, and personal development. This expansion has allowed for greater diversity and inclusivity in the types of stories and perspectives shared through podcasting.

Growth in international markets: While podcasting has its roots in the United States, it has become a global phenomenon. According to a report by Reuters, the number of people who listen to podcasts at least once a month in China has doubled over the past three years. In India, the number of podcast listeners is expected to reach 17.61 million by 2023.

Advancements in technology: The development of new technologies has made it easier for people to create, distribute, and consume podcasts. For example, portable recording equipment and editing software have made it easier for individuals and small teams to produce high-quality shows. Additionally, advancements in distribution technology have made it easier for listeners to discover new shows and for creators to monetize their work.

Monetization opportunities: As podcasting has become more popular, opportunities for monetization have expanded. While advertising has traditionally been the primary means of monetizing podcasts, other models have emerged, including sponsorships, merchandise sales, and crowdfunding. These opportunities have made it possible for podcasters to earn a living from their work.

In summary, the podcasting landscape is constantly evolving. With the growth of listenership, expansion of genres, global reach, technological advancements, and increasing opportunities for monetization, podcasting is sure to continue to grow and innovate in the years to come.

Major players in the podcasting world, including platforms, hosting services, and networks

The podcasting industry has grown significantly over the past few years, with a variety of major players emerging in the space. These players include podcast hosting services, networks, and platforms, all of which play a vital role in the creation, distribution, and monetization of podcasts.

Hosting Services
Podcast hosting services provide a platform for hosting and distributing podcast episodes. They make it easy for podcasters to upload and distribute their content to popular platforms like Apple Podcasts, Spotify, and Google Podcasts. Some popular podcast hosting services include:

Buzzsprout: Buzzsprout is a podcast hosting service that offers a user-friendly platform for uploading and distributing podcast episodes.

They offer a variety of features, including advanced analytics, transcription services, and customizable podcast players.

Libsyn: Libsyn is one of the oldest podcast hosting services, having been around since 2004. They offer a variety of features, including customizable podcast websites, monetization tools, and advanced analytics.

Podbean: Podbean is a popular podcast hosting service that offers a variety of features, including customizable podcast websites, monetization tools, and advanced analytics. They also offer a built-in advertising marketplace, which allows podcasters to connect with potential sponsors.

Podcast Networks

Podcast networks are groups of podcasts that are produced by a single company or organization. They offer a variety of benefits to podcasters, including increased exposure and access to resources like production and marketing support. Some popular podcast networks include:

Radiotopia: Radiotopia is a network of independent podcasts that are produced by PRX, a nonprofit media company. The network includes popular podcasts like 99% Invisible, Criminal, and The Memory Palace.

Gimlet Media: Gimlet Media is a podcast network that was founded in 2014. The network produces a variety of popular podcasts, including Reply All, Heavyweight, and Homecoming. In 2019, Gimlet Media was acquired by Spotify, which has helped to further increase the network's exposure.

Wondery: Wondery is a podcast network that produces a variety of popular podcasts, including Dirty John, Dr. Death, and Business Wars. The network was acquired by Amazon in 2020, which has helped to further increase its reach and resources.

Podcast Platforms

Podcast platforms are the channels through which listeners access and consume podcast content. These platforms include popular players like Apple Podcasts, Spotify, and Google Podcasts, as well as smaller, more niche platforms like Stitcher and Pocket Casts.

Apple Podcasts: Apple Podcasts is one of the largest podcast platforms, with over 1.5 million shows available on the platform. The platform is built into all Apple devices and offers a variety of features, including personalized recommendations and automatic episode downloads.

Spotify: Spotify is a popular music streaming platform that has recently expanded into the podcasting space. The platform offers a variety of features, including personalized recommendations, curated playlists, and exclusive content.

Google Podcasts: Google Podcasts is a newer player in the podcasting space, having launched in 2018. The platform offers a variety of features, including personalized recommendations, automatic episode downloads, and the ability to play podcasts directly from Google search results.

Overall, the podcasting industry is a dynamic and rapidly evolving space, with new players and developments emerging all the time. By understanding the key players and trends in the industry, podcasters can stay on top of the latest developments and take advantage of new opportunities for growth and success.

Challenges and opportunities in the podcasting industry

The podcasting industry has seen incredible growth over the past few years, with millions of people tuning in to their favorite shows every day. However, as with any industry, there are challenges and opportunities that podcasters and podcasting companies must navigate in order to stay successful.

One of the biggest challenges in the podcasting industry is discoverability. With so many shows available, it can be difficult for new podcasts to stand out and attract listeners. This is especially true for independent podcasters who may not have the marketing budget or resources of larger podcast networks. As a result, many podcasts struggle to gain traction and build a following.

Another challenge facing the industry is monetization. While there are many ways to make money from podcasting, such as sponsorships, advertising, and merchandise sales, it can be difficult for smaller podcasts to generate revenue. Additionally, there is no one-size-fits-all solution for monetization, and each podcast must find a strategy that works for them.

Despite these challenges, there are also many opportunities in the podcasting industry. One of the biggest is the growing popularity of podcasting. As more people discover and listen to podcasts, there is a growing market for new shows and a greater demand for high-quality content. This presents an opportunity for podcasters to grow their audiences and potentially earn revenue through sponsorships and advertising.

Another opportunity in the podcasting industry is the increasing number of platforms and hosting services available to podcasters. While Apple Podcasts has traditionally dominated the market, there are now a variety of platforms, such as Spotify and Stitcher, that offer podcasters alternative ways to distribute their shows. Additionally, there are a number of hosting services that provide podcasters with the tools and resources they need to create and publish their content.

In conclusion, while there are challenges and opportunities in the podcasting industry, the overall outlook is positive. With a growing audience and a wide range of platforms and hosting services available, there has never been a better time to get involved in podcasting. However, to be successful, podcasters and podcasting companies must be willing to navigate the challenges of discoverability and monetization while taking advantage of the opportunities presented by this rapidly growing industry.

PART 2:
GETTING STARTED

CHAPTER 5: WHY START A PODCAST?

❖ Benefits of podcasting as a medium for communication and entertainment

❖ How podcasting can help you reach new audiences and establish yourself as an expert in your field

❖ Examples of successful podcasts and how they have helped individuals and businesses achieve their goals

In this chapter, we'll explore the reasons why more and more people are starting their own podcasts. We'll cover the benefits of podcasting as a medium for communication and entertainment, and how it can help you reach new audiences and establish yourself as an expert in your field. We'll also look at some examples of successful podcasts and how they have helped individuals and businesses achieve their goals. Whether you're thinking about starting a podcast as a hobby or as part of your business strategy, this chapter will provide you with a solid understanding of why podcasting has become such a popular and effective way to connect with audiences.

Benefits of podcasting as a medium for communication and entertainment

Podcasting has become an increasingly popular medium for communication and entertainment in recent years. The rise of podcasts can be attributed to the many benefits the medium provides, both for listeners and creators alike.

First and foremost, podcasting allows for a high degree of flexibility in terms of content creation and consumption. With the wide range of topics and formats available, there is something for everyone in the world of podcasting. This flexibility also extends to the convenience of consuming podcasts. Listeners can choose to download and listen to podcasts at their own pace, without being tied to a specific schedule or location.

In addition, podcasting provides a unique level of intimacy between hosts and their audiences. Unlike traditional media such as television or radio, podcasts are often produced by individuals or small teams who develop a relationship with their listeners. This connection can lead to a greater sense of loyalty and engagement from listeners, as well as the potential for a stronger community around the podcast.

Podcasting is also an ideal medium for niche audiences. Traditional media may not offer content that caters to specific interests or demographics, but with podcasting, creators can tailor their content to a very specific audience. This allows for a more engaged and invested listenership that can translate into loyal fans.

For businesses, podcasting offers a unique opportunity to connect with customers and potential customers on a more personal level. Companies can use podcasts to tell their story, share their values, and offer insights into their industry. By providing valuable and informative content, businesses can build a relationship of trust with their listeners that can ultimately lead to increased brand recognition and customer loyalty.

Podcasting also offers the potential for monetization. While not all podcasts are profitable, there are a variety of ways to make money through sponsorships, advertising, merchandise sales, and more. For individuals and businesses looking to monetize their content, podcasting can be a highly effective way to do so.

Finally, podcasting allows for a level of creativity that is not always possible in other forms of media. With the freedom to choose their own topics, formats, and approaches, creators can experiment and innovate in ways that may not be possible in more traditional media settings.

In conclusion, the benefits of podcasting as a medium for communication and entertainment are clear. With flexibility, intimacy, niche audiences, business opportunities, monetization potential, and creative freedom, it's no wonder that podcasting has become such a popular medium in recent years.

How podcasting can help you reach new audiences and establish yourself as an expert in your field

Podcasting is a powerful tool for reaching new audiences and establishing yourself as an expert in your field. With its unique ability to create personalized, engaging content, podcasting offers a variety of benefits for individuals and businesses alike. In this chapter, we'll explore how podcasting can help you reach new audiences and establish yourself as an expert in your field.

Reach New Audiences
One of the most significant benefits of podcasting is its ability to reach new audiences. With podcasting, you can create personalized, engaging content that speaks directly to your target audience. By creating content that resonates with your listeners, you can build a loyal following that will help you to grow your brand and increase your reach.

Establish Yourself as an Expert
Another benefit of podcasting is its ability to establish you as an expert in your field. By sharing your knowledge and expertise with your listeners, you can build trust and credibility with your audience. This, in turn, can help you to grow your influence and establish yourself as a thought leader in your industry.

Build Brand Awareness
Podcasting is an excellent way to build brand awareness and promote your business. By creating content that is engaging, informative, and entertaining, you can increase your visibility and attract new customers to your business. With podcasting, you can

create a unique voice for your brand and establish yourself as a leader in your industry.

Connect with Your Audience

Podcasting offers a unique opportunity to connect with your audience on a personal level. By creating content that speaks directly to your listeners, you can build a strong bond with your audience and establish a sense of community around your brand. This, in turn, can help you to grow your influence and establish yourself as a leader in your industry.

Increase Engagement

Podcasting is an excellent way to increase engagement with your audience. By creating engaging, high-quality content, you can encourage your listeners to interact with your brand and share your content with others. This, in turn, can help you to increase your reach and grow your influence in your industry.

In conclusion, podcasting offers a variety of benefits for individuals and businesses looking to reach new audiences and establish themselves as experts in their field. By creating engaging, personalized content, you can build brand awareness, establish credibility, and connect with your audience on a personal level. With its unique ability to create a sense of community around your brand, podcasting is a powerful tool for growing your influence and establishing yourself as a leader in your industry.

Examples of successful podcasts and how they have helped individuals and businesses achieve their goals

Podcasts have become a popular and effective medium for businesses and individuals to reach new audiences and achieve their goals. Many successful podcasts have inspired and entertained listeners while also delivering valuable content that has helped them grow their businesses, advance their careers, or achieve personal goals.

One example of a successful podcast is "The Tim Ferriss Show." Hosted by entrepreneur and author Tim Ferriss, this podcast features interviews with successful individuals from various fields, such as business, sports, and entertainment. The podcast has been downloaded millions of times, and Ferriss has used it to establish himself as an expert in personal development and productivity. His guests often share their own insights and strategies for success, which has helped listeners gain new perspectives and ideas for their own lives and businesses.

Another successful podcast is "Serial," a true-crime podcast that became a cultural phenomenon. Hosted by journalist Sarah Koenig, the podcast investigated the 1999 murder of a high school student and raised questions about the legal system and the nature of truth. "Serial" was downloaded more than 100 million times and became the first podcast to win a Peabody Award. Its success has since spawned many other true-crime podcasts and shows.

For businesses, podcasts can also be a valuable tool for building brand awareness and attracting new customers. For example, the skincare brand Glossier launched a podcast called "The Beauty Group" to share tips and insights on beauty and skincare. The podcast has helped Glossier establish a loyal following and build a community of customers who share the brand's values and interests.

In addition to business and personal goals, podcasts can also help bring important issues to light and promote social change. "Pod Save America" is a political podcast that was created by former Obama staffers to engage and inform young people about current events and politics. The podcast has since grown into a media company that produces several other popular political podcasts and has become a powerful voice in American politics.

Overall, the success of these podcasts and many others demonstrate the power of podcasting as a medium for communication and entertainment. Through podcasts, individuals and businesses can reach new audiences, establish themselves as experts, and make a meaningful impact in their communities and the world.

CHAPTER 6: DEFINING YOUR PODCAST NICHE

- ❖   What is a podcast niche and why is it important?
- ❖   How to identify your target audience and their interests
- ❖   Strategies for choosing a podcast topic and defining your niche
- ❖   Brainstorming Your Podcast Ideas
- ❖   Examples of successful podcasts with well-defined niches

When it comes to starting a successful podcast, identifying your niche is a critical step. Your podcast niche is the specific area or topic that your podcast will focus on, and it's what sets your podcast apart from others. By defining your podcast niche, you can better target your audience and create content that appeals to their specific interests.

In this chapter, we'll explore the importance of identifying your podcast niche and target audience. We'll discuss strategies for choosing a podcast topic and defining your niche, including ways to brainstorm podcast ideas. Additionally, we'll look at examples of successful podcasts with well-defined niches to give you some inspiration and guidance.

Whether you're new to podcasting or looking to refine your podcasting strategy, this chapter will help you define your niche and create content that resonates with your target audience. So let's get started and begin brainstorming your podcast ideas!

What is a podcast niche and why is it important?

When starting a podcast, one of the most important decisions you'll need to make is defining your podcast niche. Your niche is the specific topic or area that your podcast will cover. It's what makes your podcast unique and gives it focus. In this chapter, we'll discuss what a podcast niche is, why it's important, and how to define your own.

What is a podcast niche?

A podcast niche is a specific topic or theme that your podcast will focus on. It's what sets your podcast apart from others and gives it a unique perspective. Some examples of podcast niches include true crime, personal finance, self-help, and pop culture. Your niche can be broad or narrow, but it should be specific enough to attract a dedicated audience.

Why is it important to have a podcast niche?

Defining your podcast niche is important for several reasons. First, it helps you establish your podcast's brand and identity. When you have a clearly defined niche, you can create a brand that appeals to a specific audience. This will help you attract listeners who are interested in your content and are more likely to become loyal fans.

Second, having a niche makes it easier for potential listeners to find your podcast. When people are searching for podcasts to listen to, they often search for specific topics or areas of interest. If your podcast has a clearly defined niche, it's more likely to show up in search results for those topics.

Finally, having a niche helps you create content that is focused and targeted. When you know exactly what your podcast is about, you can create episodes that are tailored to your audience's interests. This can help you establish yourself as an expert in your field and build a reputation as a go-to source for information on your niche topic.

How to define your podcast niche

Defining your podcast niche can be a challenging process, but it's important to get it right. Here are some tips to help you define your podcast niche:

Identify your interests and expertise: Start by brainstorming topics that you're passionate about and knowledgeable in. This can help you identify potential niches that you would enjoy exploring in your podcast.

Research your competition: Take a look at other podcasts in your potential niche to see what they're doing well and where there are gaps in the market. This can help you identify opportunities to create content that is unique and valuable.

Consider your audience: Think about who your target audience is and what they're interested in. This can help you identify niches that will appeal to your ideal listener.

Test your idea: Before committing to a niche, consider testing it with a few episodes or a pilot. This can help you see if your idea resonates with your audience and if there's enough interest to sustain a long-term podcast.

In conclusion, defining your podcast niche is a critical step in building a successful podcast. By choosing a specific topic or theme, you can create a brand that appeals to a dedicated audience, make it easier for potential listeners to find your podcast, and create focused, targeted content that establishes you as an expert in your field.

How to identify your target audience and their interests

In order to create a successful podcast, it's important to have a clear understanding of your target audience and their interests. Without this understanding, you risk producing content that is irrelevant to your potential listeners and will not attract a loyal following. Here are some steps you can take to identify your target audience and their interests:

Define your podcast's topic: Your podcast topic should be clear and specific. Think about what you are passionate about, what you have expertise in, and what topics would be of interest to your potential listeners.

Research your target audience: Look for data and insights about your potential listeners. You can use tools like Google Analytics, social media insights, and survey tools to gather information about your target audience's demographics, interests, and habits.

Consider your competition: Look at other podcasts in your niche and analyze their listenership. This can help you identify gaps in the market and determine what content is missing that you could provide.

Create a listener persona: Based on your research, create a profile of your ideal listener. Consider their age, gender, location, occupation, interests, and hobbies. This will help you create content that resonates with them.

Test your concept: Before launching your podcast, test your concept with a small group of your target audience. Get their feedback on your proposed topic, format, and content to ensure that it meets their needs and interests.

By taking the time to identify your target audience and their interests, you can create a podcast that is tailored to their needs and will attract a loyal following. This will help you establish yourself as an expert in your field and increase your influence and credibility within your industry.

Strategies for choosing a podcast topic and defining your niche

Once you have decided to start a podcast, one of the most important steps is defining your niche. Your niche is the area of focus for your podcast, the topic that you will be covering in each episode.

This is an essential step that will help you attract and retain listeners, establish your brand, and stand out from the competition.

Here are some strategies to help you choose a podcast topic and define your niche:

Identify your interests and expertise: Start by thinking about your interests and what you are knowledgeable about. Choose a topic that you are passionate about and that you can speak confidently and authoritatively on. This will help you create compelling content and establish yourself as an expert in your niche.

Research your competition: Look at other podcasts in your chosen niche and study their approach, format, and content. Identify gaps and opportunities that you can leverage to differentiate yourself and offer something unique to your listeners.

Narrow down your topic: Don't try to cover too many topics in one podcast. Instead, focus on a specific aspect of your niche and develop your content around it. For example, if your niche is fitness, you could create a podcast on running or weightlifting rather than covering all aspects of fitness.

Define your target audience: Identify who your ideal listener is and what their interests and needs are. Develop content that resonates with them and addresses their pain points. This will help you attract and retain listeners and build a loyal community around your podcast.

Test your topic: Before you launch your podcast, test your topic with a small group of listeners. Get their feedback and refine your approach based on their input. This will help you ensure that you are delivering content that resonates with your target audience.

By following these strategies, you can choose a podcast topic and define your niche that will help you stand out from the competition, attract and retain listeners, and establish yourself as an expert in your field. Remember to be flexible and adaptable as your niche evolves, and always keep your target audience in mind as you create content.

Brainstorming Your Podcast Ideas

Once you have identified your podcast niche and the target audience you want to reach, it's time to brainstorm podcast ideas that fit within your niche and align with your interests and expertise. Brainstorming is an essential step in the podcasting process and can help you come up with a clear and compelling concept for your show.

Here are some strategies to help you brainstorm your podcast ideas:

Brainstorm with a team: If you're planning to host your podcast with a team, it's essential to brainstorm together. Gather your team and encourage everyone to share their ideas. Brainstorming as a team can help you generate more ideas and foster creative thinking.

Research your niche: Before you start brainstorming, research your niche thoroughly. Look for similar podcasts to get inspiration and ideas. Check out what topics are trending and what your target audience is interested in. Use this information to develop your own unique angle and approach.

Identify your strengths and passions: Your podcast should reflect your passions and interests. Make a list of topics that excite you and that you have expertise in. Don't be afraid to get creative and think outside the box. The more passionate and knowledgeable you are about your topic, the more engaging and authentic your podcast will be.

Use mind mapping: Mind mapping is a visual brainstorming tool that can help you generate new ideas and make connections between them. Start with a central idea or topic and branch out with related subtopics. Keep adding subtopics until you have a comprehensive list of potential podcast ideas.

Consider your audience: Your podcast is for your audience, so consider their needs and interests when brainstorming. What do they want to learn, hear, or be entertained by? What questions do they have? Use this information to come up with relevant topics that will appeal to your target audience.

Experiment with different formats: The format of your podcast is just as important as the topic. Experiment with different formats to find what works best for your niche and audience. Do you want to do interviews, solo episodes, or a mix of both? Do you want to focus on storytelling, education, or entertainment? The format of your podcast will depend on your topic and target audience.

Remember, the goal of brainstorming is to generate as many ideas as possible, so don't worry about evaluating them at this stage. Once you have a list of potential podcast ideas, you can evaluate them based on their feasibility, originality, and relevance to your niche and target audience.

In the next chapter, we'll discuss how to choose a podcast format that fits your niche and aligns with your goals.

Examples of successful podcasts with well-defined niches

One of the keys to creating a successful podcast is defining your niche and targeting a specific audience. By focusing on a particular topic and audience, you can establish yourself as an expert and build a loyal following. Here are some examples of successful podcasts with well-defined niches:

Serial
Hosted by Sarah Koenig, Serial is a true crime podcast that tells a single story over the course of a season. Each season focuses on a

different case and explores it in depth, using interviews, archival footage, and other sources. By focusing on a specific genre and storytelling format, Serial has become one of the most popular podcasts in the world.

The Daily

Produced by The New York Times, The Daily is a news podcast that covers the most important stories of the day. Hosted by Michael Barbaro, the podcast features interviews with Times reporters and other experts, and provides a deep dive into the news. By focusing on a specific audience (people who want to stay informed about the news) and providing high-quality, in-depth reporting, The Daily has become a must-listen for many.

How I Built This

Hosted by Guy Raz, How I Built This is a podcast that interviews successful entrepreneurs and explores the stories behind their businesses. By focusing on the entrepreneurial journey, How I Built This has become a go-to resource for people who want to start their own businesses or learn from the experiences of others.

Hardcore History

Hosted by Dan Carlin, Hardcore History is a podcast that explores historical events and figures in depth. By focusing on a specific genre (history) and using a unique storytelling format that combines drama, humor, and detailed research, Hardcore History has become one of the most popular history podcasts in the world.

Stuff You Should Know

Hosted by Josh Clark and Chuck Bryant, Stuff You Should Know is a podcast that explores a wide range of topics, from science and technology to culture and history. By focusing on a broad range of subjects and providing engaging, informative content, Stuff You Should Know has become one of the most popular podcasts in the world.

These are just a few examples of successful podcasts with well-defined niches. By focusing on a specific audience, topic, or genre, these podcasts have been able to build a loyal following and establish themselves as experts in their respective fields. Whether you're starting a new podcast or looking to grow an existing one, defining your niche is a crucial step in achieving success.

CHAPTER 7: CHOOSING A PODCASTING FORMAT

- ❖ Overview of common podcasting formats, including interview, solo, and narrative styles
- ❖ How to choose a format that aligns with your goals and audience
- ❖ Pros and cons of different podcasting formats
- ❖ Examples of successful podcasts with different formats

One of the most important decisions you'll make when creating a podcast is choosing the right format. The format you choose will affect not only the way you present your content but also the audience you attract and the goals you achieve. In this chapter, we'll explore the most common podcasting formats, including interview, solo, and narrative styles, and help you decide which one is best for your podcast. We'll also discuss the pros and cons of each format and provide examples of successful podcasts that use them, including Grant Cardone's "The Cardone Zone." By the end of this chapter, you'll have a clear understanding of how to choose a format that aligns with your goals and resonates with your audience.

Overview of common podcasting formats, including interview, solo, and narrative styles

One of the great things about podcasting is the flexibility it offers in terms of content format. There are many different ways to structure a podcast, depending on the goals of the show and the preferences of the host(s). In this chapter, we will provide an overview of some of the most common podcast formats, including interview, solo, and narrative styles.

Interview-style podcasts

Interview-style podcasts are one of the most popular formats in the podcasting world. These shows feature a host who interviews guests on a specific topic or theme. The host typically prepares a list of questions for the guest(s) in advance, and the conversation is recorded and edited before being released to listeners.

Interview-style podcasts are a great way to introduce new voices and perspectives to your audience, and they can help you establish yourself as an expert in a particular field. They are also a great way to build relationships with other experts and influencers in your industry.

Solo-style podcasts

Solo-style podcasts are just what they sound like: shows in which a single host delivers content directly to the audience. These shows can take many forms, including educational or instructional podcasts, personal development shows, and commentary on current events or pop culture.

Solo-style podcasts are a great way to build a personal brand and establish yourself as an authority in your field. They can also be easier to produce than interview-style shows, since there is no need to coordinate schedules with guests.

Narrative-style podcasts

Narrative-style podcasts tell a story over the course of several episodes. This format is popular in true crime, history, and fiction genres. These shows typically involve extensive research, writing, and production, and can take several months to create.

Narrative-style podcasts are a great way to engage listeners and create a strong emotional connection with your audience. They require a significant investment of time and resources, but can be incredibly rewarding for both the host and the audience.

Hybrid podcasts

Many podcasts combine elements of different formats to create a unique listening experience. For example, an interview-style podcast might include segments of solo commentary from the host, or a narrative-style podcast might include interviews with experts or witnesses to a particular event.

Hybrid podcasts offer the flexibility to create a show that meets your specific goals and audience needs. They can also help keep your content fresh and engaging by incorporating a variety of different elements.

In conclusion, choosing the right podcast format is essential for creating a successful show that resonates with your audience. Whether you choose to go with an interview-style, solo-style, narrative-style, or hybrid format, it's important to consider your goals, audience, and resources when making your decision. With the right format in place, you can create a show that delivers high-quality content and builds a loyal following of listeners.

How to choose a format that aligns with your goals and audience

When it comes to podcasting, there are several different formats to choose from. Each format has its own unique advantages and disadvantages, and the format you choose will depend largely on your goals and the needs and interests of your audience.

Here are some of the most common podcast formats:

Interview format: In this format, the host invites a guest onto the show to discuss a specific topic. This format can be effective for building relationships with other industry experts and providing valuable insights and information to your listeners.

Solo format: In the solo format, the host speaks directly to the audience without any guests. This can be a great format for establishing yourself as an authority in your field and providing your own perspective on a particular topic.

Co-hosted format: In the co-hosted format, the show is hosted by two or more people who take turns leading the discussion. This format can be a great way to bring in multiple perspectives and provide lively conversation for your listeners.

Roundtable format: The roundtable format involves a panel of experts or guests who engage in a discussion on a particular topic. This format can be effective for providing in-depth analysis and thoughtful commentary on a specific issue.

Narrative format: The narrative format involves telling a story or following a specific storyline over the course of several episodes. This format can be a powerful tool for creating a strong emotional connection with your listeners and keeping them engaged over the long term.

Choosing the right format for your podcast will depend on a number of factors, including your goals, the interests of your audience, and your own personal style. If you are looking to establish yourself as an authority in your field, the solo format may be the best option for you. If you want to provide a lively discussion and a variety of perspectives, the co-hosted or roundtable format may be a better choice.

When choosing a format, it's important to consider the needs and interests of your audience. If you are targeting a younger demographic, for example, you may want to consider a more conversational format that is easy to listen to and engages the listener. On the other hand, if you are targeting a more professional audience, you may want to consider a more in-depth, analytical format that provides a high level of detail and expertise.

Ultimately, the key to choosing the right format for your podcast is to experiment and see what works best for you and your audience.

Whether you choose to go with an interview format, a solo format, or something else entirely, the most important thing is to create content that is engaging, informative, and valuable to your listeners.

Pros and cons of different podcasting formats

Podcasting has become an increasingly popular form of media over the years, with a wide variety of formats available for creators to choose from. Each format has its own unique advantages and disadvantages, and it's important to choose the one that aligns with your goals and target audience.

One of the most common podcast formats is the interview style, where the host talks to a guest or group of guests about a particular topic. This format is great for creating engaging content, as it allows for diverse perspectives and opinions to be shared. It can also be a great way to attract new listeners who are interested in the guests or the topics they discuss. However, the success of this format heavily relies on the quality of the guests and the questions asked by the host. If the guests are not engaging or the host's questions are not thought-provoking, listeners may lose interest quickly.

Another popular format is the solo podcast, where the host speaks directly to the audience about a particular topic or theme. This format is great for establishing the host as an expert in their field and building a personal connection with listeners. It can also be easier to produce, as it doesn't require coordinating guests or dealing with the technical difficulties that can arise during an interview. However, solo podcasts can be challenging to make engaging, as it relies solely on the host's ability to captivate the audience with their storytelling and personality.

Narrative-style podcasts, which often include elements of storytelling, sound design, and music, have also grown in popularity in recent years. This format is great for creating immersive and compelling content that can captivate listeners for long periods of time. It's also a great way to create a unique and memorable experience for your audience. However, producing narrative-style podcasts can be time-consuming and resource-intensive, as it requires a high level of production quality and attention to detail.

Other podcast formats include roundtable discussions, debates, news analysis, and hybrid formats that blend two or more styles. Each format has its own unique set of advantages and disadvantages, and it's important to choose one that aligns with your goals and target audience.

When choosing a podcast format, consider your goals for the podcast, your target audience, and the resources you have available to produce it. Think about what type of content would resonate with your audience, and what format would best showcase your unique strengths as a creator. With the right format in place, you can create engaging and compelling content that resonates with your audience and helps you achieve your goals.

Examples of successful podcasts with different formats

One of the great things about podcasting is that it allows for a wide variety of formats, each with their own unique benefits and challenges. Here are a few examples of successful podcasts with different formats:

Interview Format: "Armchair Expert with Dax Shepard"
The interview format is one of the most popular formats for podcasts, and "Armchair Expert with Dax Shepard" is a prime example of its success. Hosted by actor and comedian Dax Shepard, the show features interviews with a wide range of guests, from fellow celebrities to experts in various fields. Shepard's laid-back and conversational approach creates an intimate and entertaining atmosphere, and the diverse range of guests keeps the show fresh and interesting.

Solo Format: "The Tim Ferriss Show"
The solo format, in which a single host delivers content without a co-host or guests, can be challenging to pull off successfully, but "The

Tim Ferriss Show" demonstrates its potential. Hosted by author and entrepreneur Tim Ferriss, the show features Ferriss sharing his insights on a variety of topics related to personal development, entrepreneurship, and more. Ferriss's engaging speaking style and the depth of his knowledge keep listeners coming back for more.

Narrative Format: "Serial"

The narrative format is a great choice for storytelling, and "Serial" is widely regarded as the podcast that brought this format into the mainstream. The show's first season tells the story of a murder case in intricate detail, with host Sarah Koenig taking listeners through the twists and turns of the investigation. The show's gripping narrative, engaging host, and high production values make it a standout example of the narrative format's potential.

Hybrid Format: "The Cardone Zone"

Some podcasts use a hybrid format that combines elements of different formats to create something unique. "The Cardone Zone," hosted by entrepreneur and motivational speaker Grant Cardone, is a great example of this approach. The show features Cardone delivering solo monologues on topics related to business and personal development, as well as interviews with guests and Q&A sessions with listeners. The combination of these elements allows the show to cover a wide range of topics while keeping things fresh and engaging for listeners.

Pros and Cons of Different Formats

When choosing a podcast format, it's important to consider the pros and cons of each. Here are a few things to keep in mind:

Interview Format: Pros - Guests bring fresh perspectives and expertise, providing valuable content and helping to establish credibility. Cons - Finding and booking guests can be time-consuming and challenging, and hosts may need to adapt their style to fit the guest's personality and expertise.

Solo Format: Pros - Hosts have complete control over the content and pacing of the show, and can establish themselves as experts in their field. Cons - The lack of a co-host or guests can make it challenging to keep the show engaging, and hosts may need to work harder to keep the content fresh and interesting.

Narrative Format: Pros - The storytelling format can be incredibly engaging and powerful, drawing in listeners with a compelling narrative. Cons - The level of production required to create a high-quality narrative podcast can be time-consuming and expensive.

Hybrid Format: Pros - The combination of different formats allows for a wide range of content and keeps the show fresh and engaging. Cons - The show may feel disjointed or unfocused if the different elements don't work well together.

Choosing a Format that Aligns with Your Goals and Audience

When choosing a podcast format, it's important to consider your goals and your audience's preferences. If your goal is to establish yourself as an expert.

CHAPTER 8: PLANNING YOUR PODCAST EPISODES

❖ Why planning is important for creating a successful podcast

❖ How to plan your podcast episodes, including selecting topics, researching, outlining, and scripting

❖ Strategies for creating compelling and engaging content

❖ Tips for incorporating audience feedback into your podcast

Planning is a critical component of creating a successful podcast. Without a clear plan, your podcast can lack direction, consistency, and overall quality. In this chapter, we will discuss the importance of planning and how it can help you create compelling and engaging content that resonates with your audience.

We will explore how to plan your podcast episodes, including selecting topics, researching, outlining, and scripting. Additionally, we will provide tips and strategies for creating content that captures and retains your listeners' attention. Finally, we will discuss the importance of incorporating audience feedback into your podcast and how it can help you improve your content and grow your audience. By the end of this chapter, you will have the tools and knowledge you need to create a podcast that stands out and achieves your goals.

Why Planning is Important for Creating a Successful Podcast

Creating a podcast requires more than just pressing the record button and hoping for the best. Planning is essential to ensure a successful outcome. In this chapter, we will discuss why planning is important for creating a successful podcast.

Defines the Purpose of Your Podcast

Planning helps define the purpose of your podcast. You need to know why you're creating a podcast, who it is for, and what you want to achieve. Having a clear purpose allows you to create content that resonates with your audience and keeps them coming back for more.

Helps You Stay on Track

Planning helps you stay on track and avoid wandering aimlessly from episode to episode. By defining the topics, you want to cover, you can keep your content focused and aligned with your goals.

Provides a Framework for Content Creation

Creating content for your podcast can be overwhelming, but planning helps you create a framework for content creation. By outlining the topics you want to cover and breaking them down into sub-topics, you can ensure that you have enough content to sustain your podcast.

Ensures Consistency

Consistency is crucial for building and retaining an audience. Planning your podcast in advance helps ensure consistency in your publishing schedule, format, and content quality.

Helps You Measure Success

Planning helps you set goals and measure success. By defining what success looks like for your podcast, you can track progress, make adjustments, and improve your performance over time.

In conclusion, planning is a critical component of creating a successful podcast. It provides a roadmap for content creation, helps you stay on track, ensures consistency, and allows you to measure success. Without a plan, it's easy to get sidetracked, lose sight of your goals, and miss out on the benefits of podcasting.

How to plan your podcast episodes, including selecting topics, researching, outlining, and scripting

When it comes to creating a successful podcast, planning is a crucial step in the process. Planning your podcast episodes ensures that you have a clear vision for each episode, and that you can deliver content that engages your audience and meets your goals. In this chapter, we will explore the different steps involved in planning a podcast episode, including selecting topics, researching, outlining, and scripting.

Selecting Topics

The first step in planning your podcast episodes is to select a topic. It's essential to choose topics that align with your niche and appeal to your target audience. Start by brainstorming potential topics that you are passionate about or that you think your audience would find interesting. Consider conducting research to see what topics are currently trending in your niche or what questions your audience is asking.

Researching

Once you have selected a topic, it's time to start researching. Researching helps you gather information that you can use to create an engaging and informative podcast episode. It's essential to use reliable sources for your research and to fact-check all information. Consider using a variety of sources, such as books, articles, podcasts, and interviews with experts in your field.

Outlining

After you have completed your research, the next step is to create an outline for your podcast episode. An outline is a roadmap for your episode and helps you organize your thoughts and ideas. A basic outline includes an introduction, main points, and a conclusion. Each of these sections can be broken down further to provide more detail.

Scripting

Once you have completed your outline, you can start scripting your podcast episode. Scripting helps you ensure that your content is clear, concise, and engaging. It's essential to write your script in a conversational tone and to avoid using jargon or technical terms that your audience might not understand. Your script should include a strong introduction that hooks your audience, engaging content, and a clear conclusion that summarizes your main points.

Practice and Review

After you have scripted your podcast episode, take some time to practice delivering your content. Practicing helps you identify any areas that need improvement and ensures that you deliver your content in a confident and engaging way. Consider asking a friend or colleague to listen to your practice episodes and provide feedback.

Conclusion

Planning your podcast episodes is essential to creating a successful podcast. It helps you create engaging content that aligns with your niche and meets your audience's needs. By following the steps outlined in this chapter, you can select topics, conduct research, create an outline and script, and practice delivering your content. With a well-planned and executed podcast, you can engage your audience and achieve your goals.

Strategies for creating compelling and engaging content

Creating compelling and engaging content is crucial to the success of your podcast. Your listeners are looking for high-quality and valuable information that will entertain, educate, or inspire them. Here are some strategies to help you create content that will keep your audience coming back for more.

Start with a strong hook

Your listeners will decide within the first few seconds whether they want to keep listening or not. So, it's essential to start your episode with a strong hook that will capture their attention and make them curious about what's to come. You could begin with a surprising fact, a personal story, or a provocative question that will pique your listeners' interest.

Use storytelling techniques

Humans are wired to love stories. When you tell a story, your listeners can connect with your message on a deeper level, and it becomes more memorable. Use storytelling techniques such as creating relatable characters, a clear plotline, and a resolution to keep your audience engaged.

Be authentic

Your listeners want to connect with you, the host, as well as the content you're sharing. Don't be afraid to be yourself and share your personality and perspective on the topic you're discussing. Your authenticity will help you build a loyal audience who trusts you and your message.

Provide value

Your listeners are giving you their time, so it's important to make sure that every episode provides value. Whether it's teaching them something new, entertaining them, or inspiring them, your content should be useful and relevant to your audience.

Break it down

If your topic is complex, consider breaking it down into smaller, more digestible parts. Use clear language and avoid jargon to help your listeners understand the information you're sharing. Breaking your content down will help your listeners stay engaged and prevent them from feeling overwhelmed.

Use different formats

Variety is the spice of life, and it's no different with podcasts. Consider using different formats to keep your listeners engaged. For example, you could switch between solo episodes and interviews, or add segments such as a Q&A or a listener feedback section.

Edit your episodes

Editing your episodes will help you remove any mistakes or dead air and make your content more polished and professional. It's also an opportunity to add sound effects, music, or other creative elements that will enhance the listening experience for your audience.

Promote your content
Creating great content is just the first step; you also need to make sure that people can find it. Promote your podcast on social media, through email marketing, and other channels to reach a wider audience.

In conclusion, creating compelling and engaging content is crucial to the success of your podcast. By using storytelling techniques, providing value, and being authentic, you can build a loyal audience who will keep coming back for more. Remember to plan your episodes, use different formats, edit your content, and promote your podcast to reach a wider audience.

Tips for incorporating audience feedback into your podcast

One of the key benefits of podcasting is the ability to create a strong connection with your audience. However, in order to build and maintain that connection, it's important to not only create great content, but also to listen to your audience and incorporate their feedback. In this chapter, we'll explore some tips for effectively incorporating audience feedback into your podcast.

Encourage Feedback
The first step in incorporating audience feedback is to actively encourage it. Provide multiple ways for your listeners to share their thoughts, such as email, social media, or a feedback form on your website. Be sure to mention these channels frequently in your podcast and encourage listeners to share their thoughts and feedback.

Respond to Feedback
When your audience does provide feedback, it's important to respond in a timely manner. This not only shows your audience that

you value their opinions, but it also helps to build trust and credibility. Take the time to thank your listeners for their feedback and address any questions or concerns they may have.

Consider Feedback When Planning Episodes
As you plan future episodes, consider the feedback you've received from your audience. Are there certain topics that they seem particularly interested in? Are there questions or concerns that they've raised that you can address in a future episode? By incorporating feedback into your planning process, you can ensure that your content is relevant and engaging to your audience.

Feature Listener Questions or Comments
Another great way to incorporate audience feedback into your podcast is to feature listener questions or comments in your episodes. This not only shows your audience that you value their feedback, but it also provides an opportunity to address their concerns or questions directly. You could dedicate an entire segment of your podcast to answering listener questions, or you could simply incorporate a few listener comments or questions into each episode.

Take Action on Feedback
Finally, when you receive feedback from your audience, consider taking action on it. If multiple listeners have raised the same concern or suggestion, it may be worth exploring further. By taking action on feedback, you can not only improve your podcast, but also demonstrate to your audience that you value their opinions.

Incorporating audience feedback is a critical component of creating a successful podcast. By actively encouraging feedback, responding to it in a timely manner, and incorporating it into your planning and content creation process, you can build a stronger connection with your audience and create a podcast that truly resonates with your listeners.

CHAPTER 9: NAMING YOUR PODCAST

❖ Importance of choosing a catchy and memorable name for your podcast
❖ Strategies for brainstorming and selecting a name that reflects your podcast's topic and audience
❖ Tips for testing your podcast name and getting feedback from your target audience
❖ Examples of successful podcasts with unique and effective names

Importance of choosing a catchy and memorable name for your podcast

Choosing the right name for your podcast is one of the most important decisions you will make as a podcaster. Your podcast name is the first thing potential listeners will see and hear, and it can make a significant difference in whether they choose to give your podcast a listen. A great podcast name should be memorable, catchy, and descriptive of your content.

Your podcast name should also be unique and stand out from other podcasts in your niche. With so many podcasts available today, having a distinctive name can help you differentiate your podcast from others and make it more easily discoverable. A good name can help your podcast become a recognizable brand in its own right.

In this chapter, we will explore the importance of choosing a catchy and memorable name for your podcast. We will discuss the characteristics of a good podcast name, how to come up with ideas for your podcast name, and the potential legal considerations you should keep in mind when choosing a name. We will also provide examples of successful podcast names to inspire you in your naming process.

Strategies for Brainstorming and Selecting a Name for Your Podcast

When starting a podcast, one of the most important decisions you will make is choosing a name. Your podcast's name is the first thing potential listeners will see and hear, so it's important to make a strong first impression. A great podcast name can also help you stand out in a crowded field, and give listeners an idea of what they can expect from your show. In this chapter, we'll discuss some strategies for brainstorming and selecting a name that reflects your podcast's topic and audience.

Brainstorm keywords and themes
To start the process of choosing a name for your podcast, begin by brainstorming keywords and themes related to your show. Make a list of words that describe your podcast's topic, tone, and audience. Think about the problem your podcast is trying to solve, or the interest you are trying to satisfy. Also, consider the tone you want to set with your podcast - is it serious, lighthearted, educational, or entertaining?

Get feedback from your audience
One great way to generate ideas for your podcast's name is to get feedback from your audience. Ask your followers on social media or subscribers to your email list to suggest potential names for your show. Not only does this approach help you come up with new ideas, but it also engages your audience and makes them feel invested in your podcast's success.

Check for availability
When you've settled on a few potential names for your podcast, it's important to check that they're available for use. Start by doing a search on Google and other search engines to see if there are any existing podcasts or other media with the same name. You should also check that the domain name for your podcast is available, as well as social media handles.

Make it memorable

Your podcast's name should be easy to remember and easy to spell. Avoid using complicated or obscure words, as they may be difficult for listeners to remember or spell correctly when they're searching for your podcast online. Additionally, try to keep your podcast's name short and concise, so it's easy to say and share with others.

Use descriptive words

One effective way to make your podcast's name more memorable and descriptive is to use words that clearly convey the show's topic or theme. For example, if you're creating a podcast about cooking, words like "kitchen," "cuisine," or "recipe" could be incorporated into your name. Using descriptive words can also help potential listeners find your podcast when they're searching for content on their preferred topic.

Consider your branding

Your podcast's name should reflect your branding and the image you want to convey to your audience. Think about your podcast's overall style, tone, and audience, and choose a name that aligns with these factors. For example, if your podcast is serious and informative, choose a name that reflects that tone. Alternatively, if your podcast is more lighthearted and entertaining, choose a name that reflects that aspect of your show.

Don't be afraid to change

Remember, your podcast's name is not set in stone. If you find that your initial choice isn't resonating with your audience, or if you discover that there's another podcast with the same name, don't be afraid to change it. While it's important to put some thought into your podcast's name, it's more important to choose a name that accurately reflects your show and resonates with your audience.

Choosing a name for your podcast is an important decision that can impact the success of your show. By brainstorming keywords, getting feedback from your audience, and checking for availability, you can select a name that resonates with your target audience and accurately represents the content of your podcast. Once you have settled on a name, it is important to consider the branding of your podcast.

Branding your podcast involves creating a visual identity that reflects the personality and content of your show. This includes designing a logo, selecting a color palette, and creating consistent graphics for your website and social media channels.

Your podcast branding should be consistent with your chosen name and reflect the tone and values of your show. It is also important to consider how your branding will be perceived by your target audience and whether it will appeal to them.

A well-designed and consistent brand can help you establish a professional image and attract new listeners to your podcast. It can also help your show stand out among the thousands of other podcasts available.

In addition to branding, it is important to consider the overall aesthetic of your podcast. This includes selecting music, sound effects, and transitions that complement the tone and content of your show.

Music is an important element of podcasting and can set the tone for your show. It is important to select music that aligns with the topic and mood of your podcast, while also being engaging and memorable.

Sound effects and transitions can also be used to enhance the overall listening experience. They can be used to introduce segments, emphasize key points, and add variety to your show.

When selecting music and sound effects, it is important to consider copyright laws and obtain the necessary licenses or permissions. There are many websites that offer royalty-free music and sound effects that can be used in podcasts.

In conclusion, planning and creating a well-designed and engaging podcast is essential for attracting and retaining a loyal audience. By choosing a memorable name, developing a consistent brand, and selecting music and sound effects that enhance the listening experience, you can create a podcast that stands out among the crowd and leaves a lasting impression on your listeners.

Testing Your Podcast Name and Getting Feedback

Choosing a name for your podcast is an important decision that can have a significant impact on the success of your show. While you may have come up with a catchy and memorable name, it's important to test it out and get feedback from your target audience before launching your podcast. In this chapter, we'll explore tips for testing your podcast name and getting feedback from your target audience.

Share Your Podcast Name with Friends and Family
One way to test your podcast name is to share it with your friends and family. This can be a great way to get initial feedback on your name and see if it resonates with others. Ask for their honest opinions and take note of their feedback. If you notice a common theme in their feedback, it may be worth considering making some changes to your name.

Conduct a Survey
Another way to test your podcast name is to conduct a survey with your target audience. This can be done through social media, email, or other online platforms. Create a list of potential podcast names and ask your audience to rate them on a scale of 1-10 or choose their favorite. You can also include open-ended questions to get more detailed feedback.

Use Google AdWords
Google AdWords can be a great tool for testing your podcast name. Create a few different ads using your potential podcast names as the

headline. Run the ads for a few days and see which ad gets the most clicks. This can give you an idea of which name is most appealing to your target audience.

Conduct A/B Testing
A/B testing is a method of testing two different versions of something to see which one performs better. In this case, you can create two different versions of your podcast name and see which one resonates with your target audience. This can be done through email marketing or social media ads.

Consider Your Branding
When testing your podcast name, it's important to consider how it fits in with your branding. Your podcast name should be memorable and easy to pronounce, but it should also reflect your show's content and target audience. Make sure your name is consistent with your branding and overall message.

Pay Attention to SEO
Search engine optimization (SEO) is important for making sure your podcast is discoverable online. When testing your podcast name, make sure to conduct keyword research to see which terms are most commonly searched for in your niche. Use these keywords in your podcast name and description to improve your chances of being found online.

In conclusion, testing your podcast name and getting feedback from your target audience is an important part of creating a successful podcast. By sharing your name with friends and family, conducting a survey, using Google AdWords, conducting A/B testing, considering your branding, and paying attention to SEO, you can ensure that your podcast name is catchy, memorable, and resonates with your target audience.

Examples of successful podcasts with unique and effective names

Dove and Dragon Radio is an excellent example of a successful podcast with a unique and effective name. When choosing a name for your podcast, it's essential to consider the following factors:

Memorable: Your podcast name should be easy to remember, pronounce, and spell. Avoid using obscure or complicated words that might confuse your listeners or make it hard for them to find your show.

Unique: Your podcast name should stand out and differentiate your show from other podcasts. Avoid using generic names that might be confused with other shows or that might not reflect the unique qualities of your content.

Reflective of Your Brand and Content: Your podcast name should reflect your brand and the content of your show. Consider using keywords that highlight the central theme of your podcast.

Other examples of successful podcasts with unique and effective names include "My Favorite Murder," "Reply All," and "The Daily." These names stand out and reflect the content and tone of each show. "My Favorite Murder" is a true crime podcast that covers murder cases, while "Reply All" covers internet culture and technology-related topics. "The Daily" is a news podcast that provides daily updates on current events.

In conclusion, choosing a unique and effective name for your podcast is essential for capturing the attention of potential listeners and establishing your brand. When brainstorming names, consider making it memorable, unique, and reflective of your brand and content.

In conclusion, choosing the right name for your podcast is crucial for attracting listeners and building your brand. A catchy and memorable name can help your show stand out in a crowded market, while also reflecting the content and personality of your podcast.

When brainstorming a name, it's important to consider your target audience and the topics you cover in your show. You want a name that accurately represents your brand and is easy to remember and pronounce. It's also essential to test your podcast name and get feedback from your audience to ensure that it resonates with them.

As demonstrated by Dove and Dragon Radio, a unique and effective podcast name can capture listeners' attention and provide a glimpse into the hosts' personalities and the content of the show. So take the time to come up with a great name for your podcast, and you'll be one step closer to creating a successful and memorable podcast.

CHAPTER 10: DESIGNING YOUR PODCAST COVER ART

❖ The Importance of Podcast Cover Art
❖ Designing Effective Podcast Cover Art
❖ Best practices for creating high-quality podcast cover art
❖ Examples of successful podcasts with eye-catching and effective cover art

Your podcast cover art is the first thing listeners will see when browsing through podcast directories, and it can play a crucial role in attracting potential listeners and setting your show apart from the rest. In this chapter, we'll explore the importance of creating effective podcast cover art and strategies for designing a cover that reflects your podcast's brand and topic. We'll also review best practices for creating high-quality cover art that will make your podcast look professional and engaging.

The Importance of Podcast Cover Art

Podcast cover art is an essential element of any successful podcast. It's often the first thing listeners see when browsing through a podcast directory, and it can make or break the decision to listen to a show. In this chapter, we'll discuss why podcast cover art is important, how it can help you stand out in a crowded podcast landscape, and how to create compelling cover art that resonates with your audience.

Why Podcast Cover Art is Important

Podcast cover art is the visual representation of your podcast. It's the first impression that potential listeners have of your show, and it sets the tone for what they can expect to hear. The right cover art can attract listeners, while poor cover art can turn them off. In addition to attracting listeners, cover art can also help build brand recognition and loyalty. It's an opportunity to communicate your podcast's tone, style, and topic at a glance.

How Cover Art Can Help You Stand Out in a Crowded Podcast Landscape

The podcast landscape is becoming increasingly crowded, with over 2 million podcasts available worldwide. With so many options available, it's important to have a unique and eye-catching cover art that sets your podcast apart from the rest. This is especially true for new and upcoming podcasts that are still building an audience. Having a memorable and visually striking cover art can help your podcast stand out, grab attention, and make a lasting impression on potential listeners.

How to Create Compelling Cover Art

Creating compelling cover art requires thoughtful consideration of your podcast's topic, tone, and style. It should be eye-catching, memorable, and reflective of your brand. One effective strategy is to use bold and bright colors that grab the viewer's attention. Another is to incorporate your podcast's title or a relevant image that represents your show's topic. It's also important to consider the size and resolution of the image, as it needs to look sharp and professional on different platforms and devices.

Conclusion

In conclusion, podcast cover art is an essential element of any successful podcast. It's the first impression that potential listeners have of your show and sets the tone for what they can expect to hear. The right cover art can attract listeners, build brand recognition and loyalty, and help your podcast stand out in a crowded landscape. By taking the time to create compelling cover art that resonates with your audience, you can increase the chances of attracting and retaining listeners.

Designing Effective Podcast Cover Art

In the crowded podcast landscape, it's important to make your podcast stand out, and one way to do this is through effective cover art. Your podcast's cover art is often the first thing potential listeners see, so it's essential to make a strong first impression that accurately reflects your brand and topic. In this chapter, we will explore the strategies for designing effective podcast cover art.

Understand Your Brand and Audience
The first step in designing effective podcast cover art is to understand your brand and audience. Your cover art should be reflective of your podcast's brand and topic, and it should appeal to your target audience. Take some time to think about your podcast's unique value proposition, what sets it apart from other podcasts in your niche, and how you can visually communicate that through your cover art.

Keep It Simple and Eye-Catching
Your cover art needs to be eye-catching and stand out in a crowded marketplace, but it also needs to be simple and easy to read. Avoid clutter and focus on creating a clear and concise design. Use bold colors and large fonts to ensure your cover art is visible even in a small thumbnail size.

Incorporate Relevant Images or Graphics
Images and graphics can be a powerful tool for communicating your podcast's topic and brand. Consider incorporating relevant images or graphics into your cover art. For example, if you have a podcast about cooking, you might include an image of a chef's hat or a graphic of cooking utensils.

Use Consistent Branding
Consistency is key when it comes to branding, so make sure your podcast cover art is consistent with your overall branding. Use the same

colors, fonts, and imagery across all of your podcast branding to create a cohesive and recognizable brand identity.

Get Feedback and Make Adjustments
Once you have a design, it's important to get feedback from others. Share your cover art with friends, family, and potential listeners to get their opinions. Take their feedback into consideration and make adjustments as necessary.

Follow Technical Guidelines
Finally, it's important to follow technical guidelines when creating your podcast cover art. Different platforms have different requirements for size and format, so make sure you're following the guidelines for each platform where your podcast will be hosted.

In conclusion, effective podcast cover art is essential for standing out in a crowded podcast landscape. By understanding your brand and audience, keeping it simple and eye-catching, incorporating relevant images or graphics, using consistent branding, getting feedback and making adjustments, and following technical guidelines, you can design cover art that accurately reflects your podcast's brand and topic while attracting potential listeners.

Best practices for creating high-quality podcast cover art:

When it comes to creating a successful podcast, having high-quality cover art is a must. Your cover art is the first thing potential listeners will see and can be the difference between them clicking play or scrolling past. Here are some best practices for creating high-quality podcast cover art:

Keep it simple: Your cover art should be easy to read and understand at a glance. Avoid cluttered designs and too much text or imagery that can be overwhelming and confusing to potential listeners.

Use high-quality images: Your cover art should be high-resolution, clear, and easy to see. Avoid using low-quality or pixelated images that can make your podcast appear unprofessional.

Reflect your podcast's brand and topic: Your cover art should accurately reflect the theme and tone of your podcast. Use colors, fonts, and imagery that align with your brand and topic.

Consider your platform: Different platforms may display your cover art differently, so be sure to check the guidelines and size requirements for each one. Make sure your cover art is optimized for all platforms.

Test it out: Before finalizing your cover art, get feedback from your audience, friends, and colleagues. Ask for honest opinions on whether your cover art accurately reflects your podcast and if it stands out in a crowded market.

Be consistent: Once you have chosen your cover art, use it consistently across all platforms and marketing materials to build recognition and brand awareness.

Overall, creating high-quality podcast cover art takes time and effort, but it can make a significant impact on the success of your podcast. By following these best practices, you can design a cover art that accurately reflects your brand and topic, stands out in a crowded market, and entices potential listeners to give your podcast a listen.

Examples of successful podcasts with eye-catching and effective cover art:

One of the most important ways to make your podcast stand out in a crowded market is to have eye-catching and effective cover art. Your cover art is the first impression that potential listeners have of your podcast, and it can make all the difference in whether or not they decide to give your show a chance.

Here are some examples of successful podcasts with memorable and effective cover art:

"Crime Junkie" - The cover art for this true crime podcast is simple but striking. It features a magnifying glass over a black background with the show's name in bold white letters. The imagery immediately conveys the show's focus on crime and investigation, while the bold lettering ensures that the title is legible even at small sizes.

"The Daily" - The cover art for this news podcast from The New York Times is minimalistic but memorable. It features a simple blue and white color scheme with the show's name in bold capital letters. The use of the newspaper icon on the lower left corner reinforces the brand's association with The New York Times and the concept of daily news.

"How I Built This" - The cover art for this business podcast is playful and engaging. It features a hand-drawn illustration of a house with a speech bubble and the show's name in bold block letters. The imagery reflects the show's focus on entrepreneurship and the idea of building something from the ground up.

"Lore" - The cover art for this horror and folklore podcast is dark and mysterious. It features a black and white photograph of a forest with the show's name in a gothic font. The imagery immediately evokes a sense of mystery and intrigue, while the font reflects the show's focus on history and folklore.

When designing your podcast cover art, it's important to think about your show's brand and topic, and to choose imagery and typography that reflect those elements. You want your cover art to be memorable, eye-catching, and easy to read, so that potential listeners can quickly understand what your show is about and why they should listen.

In conclusion, creating effective and eye-catching cover art is an important part of building a successful podcast. By studying successful examples like "Crime Junkie," "The Daily," "How I Built This," and "Lore," you can gain inspiration for your own podcast cover art and create a visual identity that will help your show stand out in a crowded market.

Introduction:
Your podcast cover art is the first thing listeners will see when browsing through podcast directories, and it can play a crucial role in attracting potential listeners and setting your show apart from the rest. In this chapter, we'll explore the importance of creating effective podcast cover art and strategies for designing a cover that reflects your podcast's brand and topic. We'll also review best practices for creating high-quality cover art that will make your podcast look professional and engaging.

CHAPTER 11: PREPARING YOUR PODCAST LAUNCH

- ❖ How to prepare for a successful podcast launch, including setting a launch date and creating a launch strategy
- ❖ Strategies for building anticipation and excitement for your podcast before it launches
- ❖ Best practices for promoting your podcast and building an audience before and after launch
- ❖ Tips for measuring success and adjusting your launch strategy as needed

Launching a podcast can be an exciting and rewarding endeavor, but it requires more than just recording and publishing episodes. To increase your chances of success, it's important to prepare for your podcast launch and create a launch strategy that aligns with your goals and audience. In this chapter, we'll explore some strategies for building anticipation and excitement for your podcast, promoting it before and after launch, and measuring its success. Whether you're a first-time podcaster or a seasoned pro, these tips can help you increase your chances of a successful launch.

How to Prepare for a Successful Podcast Launch

Congratulations, you have worked hard to create your podcast content, chosen a name, and designed a captivating cover art. The next step is to launch your podcast to the world. Launching a podcast can be a daunting task, especially with so many podcasts already available in the market. However, with a solid launch strategy, you can stand out and attract new listeners. In this chapter, we will discuss how to prepare for a successful podcast launch, including setting a launch date and creating a launch strategy.

Setting a Launch Date

One of the first steps in launching a successful podcast is to set a launch date. This will give you a specific deadline to work towards, and also helps to build excitement and anticipation among your audience. When setting a launch date, you want to consider factors such as the production schedule, promotional efforts, and availability of guests (if you plan on having guests). It is also important to give yourself enough time to produce high-quality episodes.

Creating a Launch Strategy

Creating a launch strategy is a crucial part of preparing for a successful podcast launch. A launch strategy involves planning and executing promotional efforts that will help your podcast gain visibility and attract new listeners. Here are some strategies you can use:

Utilize Social Media - Use your social media platforms to promote your upcoming podcast launch. Share teasers, behind-the-scenes footage, and information about what your podcast will cover.

Build a Pre-Launch Email List - Build a list of email subscribers who are interested in your podcast. Share updates, sneak peeks, and other exclusive content with your email subscribers before your podcast launch.

Collaborate with Other Podcasters - Reach out to other podcasters in your niche and collaborate on an episode or promotional efforts. This can help to expand your audience and increase visibility.

Offer Exclusive Content - Offer exclusive content or early access to your podcast episodes to your email subscribers or social media followers.

Leverage Paid Advertising - Consider using paid advertising such as Facebook ads, Instagram ads, or Google ads to increase your podcast's visibility.

In conclusion, launching a successful podcast requires careful planning and execution. Setting a launch date and creating a launch strategy are important steps to prepare for a successful launch. Utilize social media, build a pre-launch email list, collaborate with other podcasters, offer exclusive content, and leverage paid advertising to increase visibility and attract new listeners. With the right launch strategy, you can stand out in a crowded podcast landscape and build a loyal following for your podcast.

Strategies for building anticipation and excitement for your podcast before it launches

Building anticipation and excitement for your podcast before it launches is a crucial step in achieving a successful launch. By creating buzz and anticipation around your show, you can generate interest and excitement that will carry over into your initial episodes and beyond. Here are some strategies for building anticipation and excitement for your podcast before it launches:

Start promoting your podcast early: It's important to start promoting your podcast well before your launch date. This can include posting teaser clips or trailers on social media, creating a landing page for your podcast, and reaching out to potential listeners and industry influencers.

Create a launch team: A launch team is a group of individuals who help promote your podcast before and during the launch. These can be family, friends, and colleagues who are excited about your podcast and willing to share it with their own networks.

Host a pre-launch event: Hosting a pre-launch event, such as a virtual Q&A or a live-streamed sneak peek, can help generate excitement and interest for your podcast. This can also help you connect with potential listeners and build relationships with your audience.

Utilize social media: Social media is a powerful tool for building anticipation and excitement for your podcast. You can use social media to share behind-the-scenes glimpses of your show, tease upcoming episodes, and engage with your audience.

Leverage your network: Don't be afraid to leverage your existing network of contacts to help promote your podcast. Reach out to other podcasters in your niche, industry influencers, and past guests to help generate buzz and excitement for your show.

By implementing these strategies, you can build anticipation and excitement for your podcast before it launches, ensuring a successful launch and a strong start to your podcasting journey.

Best practices for promoting your podcast and building an audience before and after launch

Launching a podcast is an exciting venture, but it's important to remember that your work doesn't end once your first episode goes live. In order to grow your audience and achieve long-term success, you need to promote your podcast effectively before and after launch. Here are some best practices for doing just that:

Identify your target audience: Before you can effectively promote your podcast, you need to know who your target audience is. This will inform your marketing strategies and help you tailor your content to better meet their needs and interests.

Leverage your existing network: Start by promoting your podcast to your existing network of friends, family, and colleagues. Ask them to help spread the word by sharing your podcast with their own networks. This can help create a strong initial following and generate early momentum.

Utilize social media: Social media platforms like Twitter, Facebook, and Instagram can be powerful tools for promoting your podcast. Share teasers, trailers, and other promotional content on these platforms and engage with your followers to build relationships and create buzz.

Submit your podcast to directories: There are many podcast directories and apps, such as Apple Podcasts, Spotify, and Stitcher, that can help you reach a wider audience. Submit your podcast to these directories as soon as possible and make sure your cover art and podcast description are optimized to attract listeners.

Reach out to influencers and industry experts: Consider reaching out to influencers and experts in your industry who may be interested in your podcast. Ask them to appear as a guest on your show or to promote it to their own followers.

Utilize email marketing: Email marketing can be an effective way to promote your podcast and keep your audience engaged. Build an email list of interested listeners and send regular updates and teasers to keep them excited about your upcoming episodes.

Consistency is key: Finally, remember that consistency is key when it comes to promoting your podcast. Develop a regular schedule for promoting your show and make sure you're delivering consistent, high-quality content to your listeners.

By following these best practices, you can effectively promote your podcast and build an engaged, loyal audience. Remember that podcast promotion is an ongoing process, so keep testing new strategies and refining your approach to find what works best for you and your audience.

Tips for measuring success and adjusting your launch strategy as needed

Launching a podcast can be an exciting experience, but success isn't always guaranteed. Even with careful planning and promotion, it's important to measure your podcast's success and adjust your launch strategy if necessary. In this chapter, we'll cover some tips for measuring success and adjusting your launch strategy as needed.

Track your metrics: To measure your podcast's success, you need to track your metrics. Metrics such as downloads, subscribers, and listener engagement can give you insights into how well your podcast is performing. By tracking these metrics, you can identify areas of improvement and adjust your launch strategy accordingly.

Solicit feedback: Feedback is essential for understanding your audience's needs and preferences. Encourage your listeners to leave reviews, comments, and feedback about your podcast. This feedback can help you identify areas of improvement and make changes to your launch strategy.

Monitor social media: Social media can be a great tool for building an audience and promoting your podcast. By monitoring social media, you can see how people are talking about your podcast and identify areas of opportunity for engagement. Engage with your audience on social media and use it as a tool to build relationships and gain insights into your audience's preferences.

Adjust your strategy: Based on the metrics, feedback, and social media monitoring, adjust your launch strategy as needed. If your metrics are lower than expected, identify areas for improvement and adjust your strategy accordingly. If your feedback is indicating a need for changes, make those changes. Be willing to adapt and adjust your strategy to best serve your audience and reach your goals.

Stay engaged with your audience: Even after your launch, it's important to stay engaged with your audience. Continue to solicit feedback and track your metrics to ensure your podcast is meeting your audience's needs. Use this feedback to make adjustments to your launch strategy as needed.

In conclusion, launching a successful podcast requires careful planning, promotion, and measurement. By tracking your metrics, soliciting feedback, monitoring social media, adjusting your strategy, and staying engaged with your audience, you can launch a successful podcast and adjust your launch strategy as needed. Remember, launching a podcast is a journey, and the best results come from an iterative approach that involves continuous improvement and adaptation.

Conclusion:

Launching a successful podcast takes time, effort, and planning, but the rewards can be significant. By setting a launch date, creating a launch strategy, building anticipation and excitement, promoting your podcast, and measuring your success, you can increase your chances of reaching your goals and building a loyal audience. Remember to be patient, persistent, and open to feedback and improvement, and don't be afraid to adjust your strategy as needed. With these tips and a strong commitment to your vision and values, you can make your podcast stand out in a crowded landscape and make a meaningful impact on your listeners.

CHAPTER 12: ESSENTIAL PODCASTING EQUIPMENT

❖ Overview of the essential equipment you need to start a podcast, including microphones, headphones, and recording software
❖ Strategies for choosing the right equipment for your needs and budget
❖ Best practices for setting up your recording space and configuring your equipment
❖ Examples of high-quality podcasting equipment and their features

Starting a podcast requires a certain level of investment in equipment to ensure high-quality audio production. With so many options available in the market, it can be overwhelming to know which equipment to choose. In this chapter, we will provide an overview of the essential equipment you need to start a podcast, including microphones, headphones, and recording software. We will also discuss strategies for choosing the right equipment for your needs and budget, as well as best practices for setting up your recording space and configuring your equipment.

Overview of the essential equipment you need to start a podcast, including microphones, headphones, and recording software

Starting a podcast requires some basic equipment to ensure that your audio quality is top-notch. While the right gear can enhance your podcast, you don't need to spend a fortune to get started. In this chapter, we will cover the essential equipment you need to start a podcast, including microphones, headphones, and recording software.

Microphones
A good quality microphone is essential for creating high-quality audio for your podcast. There are two main types of microphones:

dynamic and condenser. Dynamic microphones are more rugged and durable and are ideal for recording in noisy environments. They are also less expensive than condenser microphones. On the other hand, condenser microphones are more sensitive and produce high-quality audio, but they are more expensive and require a power source.

Headphones
Wearing headphones during a podcast recording session is essential to ensure that you can hear what you and your guests are saying clearly. Headphones can also prevent audio feedback, which can occur when the microphone picks up the audio output from the speakers.

Recording Software
To record and edit your podcast, you will need recording software. There are many options to choose from, but some popular ones include Audacity, GarageBand, and Hindenburg Journalist. These programs allow you to record, edit, and mix audio tracks, adjust levels, and add sound effects.

Additional Equipment
In addition to the basic equipment, there are some other pieces of equipment that you may need, depending on the format of your podcast. For example, if you plan to record interviews in person, you may need a portable audio recorder. If you plan to record with multiple guests or co-hosts, you may need an audio interface, which allows you to connect multiple microphones to your recording software.

In conclusion, investing in high-quality equipment can make a big difference in the audio quality of your podcast. While you don't need to spend a lot of money to get started, it's worth considering investing in a good quality microphone and headphones, as well as recording software to help you produce a professional-sounding podcast. By having the right equipment, you can ensure that your listeners have an enjoyable and engaging listening experience.

Strategies for choosing the right equipment for your needs and budget

When starting a podcast, one of the most important decisions you'll make is choosing the right equipment. The right equipment can make all the difference in the quality of your podcast's audio and ultimately, the success of your show. Here are some strategies for choosing the right equipment for your needs and budget.

Identify your needs: The first step in choosing the right equipment is to identify your needs. What type of podcast are you creating? Will you be recording solo or with guests? What is your budget? By answering these questions, you can narrow down your options and choose equipment that suits your needs.

Do your research: Once you've identified your needs, do some research to find out what equipment is available and what other podcasters are using. Look for reviews and recommendations from other podcasters to get a sense of what works well in your industry.

Consider your budget: Podcasting equipment can range from budget-friendly to high-end, so consider your budget when making your choices. You don't need to break the bank to get good quality equipment, but keep in mind that investing in higher-end gear can result in better audio quality and longevity.

Start with the essentials: When starting out, focus on the essentials: a good quality microphone, headphones, and recording software. You can always add more equipment later as your budget allows.

Test before you buy: Before making any purchases, test out the equipment you're considering. If possible, try before you buy to get a sense of the sound quality and ease of use.

Consider portability: If you plan to record on the go, consider portable equipment that can be easily transported. A quality portable microphone can make all the difference when recording in different environments.

Invest in a pop filter: A pop filter is an inexpensive but essential piece of equipment that can greatly improve the audio quality of your recordings. It helps to reduce popping and hissing sounds that can be caused by certain sounds and letters.

By following these strategies, you can choose equipment that meets your needs, fits your budget, and helps you create a high-quality podcast.

In conclusion, choosing the right equipment is an essential part of starting a podcast. By identifying your needs, doing your research, considering your budget, focusing on the essentials, testing before you buy, considering portability, and investing in a pop filter, you can choose equipment that helps you create a successful podcast with high-quality audio.

Best practices for setting up your recording space and configuring your equipment

When starting a podcast, it is essential to have a dedicated space for recording your episodes. This space should be quiet, well-lit, and free from distractions. Once you have your recording space set up, it's important to configure your equipment properly to ensure high-quality sound. Here are some best practices for setting up your recording space and configuring your equipment:

Choose the right space: The first step in setting up your recording space is choosing the right location. Look for a quiet, enclosed space with minimal external noise and echo. Avoid recording in large open spaces or areas with lots of hard surfaces, such as tiled floors or glass windows, as they can create unwanted echoes and reverb.

Invest in soundproofing: Soundproofing your recording space can help reduce external noise and improve the overall quality of your recordings. You can purchase acoustic foam panels, sound-absorbing blankets, or even build your own DIY soundproofing solutions.

Select the right equipment: When selecting your recording equipment, it's essential to choose a high-quality microphone, headphones, and recording software. Consider your needs and budget when making your selections, but keep in mind that the quality of your equipment will impact the overall sound of your podcast.

Position your microphone correctly: Proper microphone placement is essential for capturing clear and accurate sound. Position your microphone at the appropriate distance from your mouth and adjust the angle for optimal sound quality. A pop filter can also help reduce popping and other mouth noises.

Test and adjust your equipment: Before recording your first episode, it's essential to test your equipment and make any necessary adjustments. Listen to sample recordings and make adjustments to your microphone or recording settings as needed.

Monitor your audio levels: Keep an eye on your audio levels throughout the recording process to ensure that your sound is clear and consistent. Adjust your microphone and recording levels as needed to avoid distortion or low volume.

By following these best practices, you can ensure that your recording space and equipment are optimized for high-quality sound. With the right setup and configuration, you can produce professional-quality podcasts that are sure to engage and entertain your listeners.

Examples of high-quality podcasting equipment and their features

Smartphone: If you are on a tight budget, you can use your smartphone to record your podcast. Most smartphones have built-in microphones that are good enough for recording basic podcasts.

USB Microphone: A USB microphone is an affordable option for recording high-quality audio. They are easy to set up, and many models come with built-in pop filters to reduce unwanted noise.

XLR Microphone: XLR microphones are professional-grade microphones that require an audio interface to connect to your computer. They offer superior sound quality and are ideal for recording music or other types of high-fidelity audio.

Audio Interface: An audio interface is a device that connects your XLR microphone to your computer. It converts analog signals to digital signals and provides a preamp to boost the signal before it is recorded.

Studio Headphones: Studio headphones are designed to provide accurate sound reproduction, making them ideal for editing and mixing your podcast. They are also comfortable to wear for extended periods of time.

Studio Monitors: Studio monitors are high-quality speakers that are designed to provide accurate sound reproduction. They are essential for recording and mixing music, but they are also useful for podcasting.

Digital Audio Workstation (DAW) Software: DAW software is used to record, edit, and mix your podcast. There are many affordable options available, such as Audacity, as well as more advanced options like Pro Tools or Logic Pro.

Portable Recorder: If you plan to record your podcast on location, a portable recorder can be a great option. They are compact, battery-powered, and offer high-quality sound recording.

It's worth noting that the cost of podcasting equipment can vary greatly depending on your needs and preferences. It's important to do your research and choose the equipment that best fits your budget and production goals.

Conclusion:

Investing in quality podcasting equipment is essential for producing a high-quality show that engages and captivates your audience. By understanding the different types of equipment available and how they work together, you can create a setup that meets your specific needs and budget. By following best practices for setting up your recording space and configuring your equipment, you can ensure that your audio is of the highest quality possible. With the right equipment and setup, you can create a professional-sounding podcast that stands out in a crowded market and builds a loyal following of listeners.

CHAPTER 13: RECORDING YOUR PODCAST

❖ How to record your podcast
❖ Tips for setting up your recording space and creating a comfortable and quiet recording environment
❖ Strategies for recording high-quality audio, including microphone techniques and voice modulation
❖ Best practices for recording interviews, remote guests, and group discussions

How to record your podcast

Once you have your equipment set up and ready to go, it's time to start recording your podcast. This chapter will cover the key steps to successfully record your podcast, including selecting the right recording software and settings.

Selecting the Right Recording Software

The first step in recording your podcast is to select the right recording software. There are many recording software options available, but here are a few popular ones:

Audacity - Audacity is a free, open-source recording software that is popular among podcasters. It is available for Windows, Mac, and Linux and has a wide range of features, including the ability to record, edit, and mix audio.

GarageBand - GarageBand is a popular recording software for Mac users. It is free and has many features that are useful for podcasting, such as a variety of sound effects and built-in instruments.

Adobe Audition - Adobe Audition is a professional-level recording software that is available for both Mac and PC. It has a wide range of features, including advanced editing tools and the ability to record and edit multiple tracks.

Selecting the Right Recording Settings

Once you have selected your recording software, it's time to set up your recording settings. Here are a few key settings to consider:

Sample Rate - The sample rate is the number of times per second that the software records a sound. A higher sample rate will result in better quality audio but will also create larger file sizes. A sample rate of 44.1kHz is typically recommended for podcasting.

Bitrate - The bitrate is the amount of data that is recorded per second. A higher bitrate will also result in better quality audio but will create larger file sizes. A bitrate of 128kbps is typically recommended for podcasting.

Recording Format - The recording format is the type of file that your recording software will produce. MP3 is the most common format for podcasting, but other options include WAV and AIFF.

Recording Your Podcast

With your recording software and settings configured, it's time to start recording your podcast. Here are a few tips to keep in mind:

Test your equipment - Before you start recording your podcast, take a few minutes to test your equipment and make sure everything is working correctly.

Choose a quiet recording location - Choose a quiet location to record your podcast to minimize background noise and other distractions.

Record multiple takes - It's a good idea to record multiple takes of each segment to give yourself more options when editing.

Save your files - Save your recording files to a dedicated folder on your computer so they are easy to find and access.

In conclusion, recording your podcast can be a fun and rewarding experience. By selecting the right recording software and settings, and following best practices for recording, you can create high-quality audio that your listeners will love.

Tips for setting up your recording space and creating a comfortable and quiet recording environment

When it comes to recording your podcast, having a quiet and comfortable environment is key to producing high-quality audio. In this chapter, we'll discuss some tips for setting up your recording space and creating a comfortable environment for you to record in.

Choose a quiet location: When selecting a location for your recording space, choose a room that is quiet and free from outside noise. Avoid spaces with loud HVAC systems, high-traffic areas, or areas that have a lot of ambient noise.

Use acoustic treatment: Acoustic treatment can help reduce the amount of reverb in your recording space and improve the overall sound quality. Consider adding acoustic foam panels or sound-absorbing curtains to the walls and ceiling.

Eliminate noise: Take steps to eliminate any sources of noise in your recording space, such as turning off appliances, unplugging electronic devices that emit noise, and closing windows and doors.

Invest in a microphone stand: A microphone stand can help you maintain a consistent distance from the microphone and reduce handling noise, which can improve the sound quality of your recordings.

Use a pop filter: A pop filter can help reduce plosives and other mouth noises that can detract from the overall quality of your recording.

Adjust your seating position: Sit in a comfortable chair with good posture to prevent slouching, which can affect the sound quality of your recording. Make sure your chair is at the correct height for your recording setup.

Consider your clothing: Wear clothing that does not produce excessive noise or rustling sounds. Avoid wearing jewelry that can make noise when it comes into contact with your microphone.

By following these tips, you can set up a recording space that is quiet, comfortable, and conducive to high-quality audio recording. Remember, creating a great podcast is not just about the content, but also the quality of the audio. By investing in a good recording environment, you'll be able to produce a podcast that listeners will love.

Recording high-quality audio is crucial to the success of your podcast. Poor audio quality can be distracting and make it difficult for listeners to focus on your content. In this chapter, we'll discuss some strategies for recording high-quality audio, including microphone techniques and voice modulation.

Microphone Techniques

The quality of your microphone and how you use it can have a significant impact on the overall sound quality of your podcast. Here are some tips for getting the most out of your microphone:

Use a high-quality microphone: A high-quality microphone can make a big difference in the clarity and richness of your voice. There are many affordable options available that can produce great results.

Position your microphone correctly: The position of your microphone can affect the sound quality. Experiment with different positions to find the one that works best for your voice and recording space. A good starting point is to place the microphone about six inches away from your mouth and slightly off to one side.

Use a pop filter: A pop filter is a screen that attaches to your microphone and helps reduce popping sounds when you say words that begin with "p" or "b."

Consider using a shock mount: A shock mount is a device that suspends your microphone, which can help reduce vibrations and background noise.

Voice Modulation
The way you speak can also affect the quality of your audio. Here are some tips for improving your voice modulation:

Speak clearly and consistently: Make sure you enunciate your words clearly and consistently throughout your podcast. This will make it easier for listeners to follow along.

Vary your pitch and tone: Varying your pitch and tone can add interest and emphasis to your words. Experiment with different inflections to find what works best for your content.

Use pauses effectively: Pausing at strategic moments can help build suspense and allow your listeners to process what you've just said.

Other Tips for High-Quality Audio
Here are some other tips for recording high-quality audio:

Record in a quiet environment: Choose a quiet room to record in and close any windows or doors to block out external noise.

Minimize background noise: Turn off any electronics or appliances that could create background noise, such as fans or air conditioners.

Check your levels: Before you start recording, make sure your microphone levels are set correctly. You want to avoid clipping (when the sound is too loud and distorted) or being too quiet.

Record in short segments: Consider breaking your podcast up into shorter segments to make it easier to edit and manage.

By following these strategies for recording high-quality audio, you can ensure that your podcast sounds professional and engaging.

In the next chapter, we'll discuss some tips for editing and post-production to further enhance the quality of your podcast.

Best practices for recording interviews, remote guests, and group discussions

Recording interviews, remote guests, and group discussions is a common practice in the world of podcasting. However, these types of recordings can present unique challenges when it comes to ensuring high-quality audio. In this chapter, we'll discuss some best practices for recording interviews, remote guests, and group discussions to help you produce the best possible audio for your podcast.

Test your equipment and settings beforehand: Before you begin recording, test your equipment and settings to make sure everything is working properly. This includes testing your microphones, headphones, and recording software, as well as adjusting your recording levels and checking for any background noise or echoes.

Use a reliable internet connection: If you're recording a remote guest or conducting an interview over the internet, a reliable internet connection is essential. Test your internet connection beforehand to ensure that it is stable and fast enough to support a clear audio connection.

Use a high-quality microphone: A high-quality microphone is essential for recording clear and crisp audio. When recording interviews, remote guests, or group discussions, consider using a microphone for each person to ensure the best possible audio quality.

Control background noise: When recording interviews or group discussions, it's important to control background noise as much as possible. Choose a quiet location for your recording and consider using noise-cancelling headphones to reduce background noise.

Conduct a sound check: Before you begin recording, conduct a sound check with all participants to make sure that everyone's audio levels are balanced and that everyone is coming through clearly.

Use a recording backup: To avoid the risk of losing your recording due to technical issues, always use a recording backup. This can be as simple as recording a backup copy on a separate device or using software that automatically saves a backup copy.

Consider using a call recording software: If you're conducting remote interviews or discussions, consider using a call recording software to ensure high-quality audio. There are several options available that allow you to record calls directly from your computer, with options for high-quality audio and automatic backups.

By following these best practices for recording interviews, remote guests, and group discussions, you can ensure that your podcast episodes have high-quality audio, even when recording under less than ideal circumstances.

In conclusion, recording interviews, remote guests, and group discussions can present unique challenges for podcasters, but with the right equipment, settings, and techniques, you can produce high-quality audio that your listeners will appreciate. Whether you're recording in person or remotely, always take the time to test your equipment and settings, control background noise, and conduct a sound check to ensure that your recordings are the best they can be.

CHAPTER 14: EDITING YOUR PODCAST

❖ Why editing is important for creating a professional-sounding podcast
❖ Overview of common editing software and techniques
❖ Tips for editing your podcast to create a polished and engaging final product
❖ Strategies for incorporating music, sound effects, and other elements into your podcast

Editing is a crucial step in the podcast production process that can make or break the success of your show. It involves taking the raw audio recordings and turning them into a polished and engaging final product that listeners will love. In this chapter, we'll discuss why editing is so important for creating a professional-sounding podcast, provide an overview of common editing software and techniques, and offer tips for editing your podcast to make it the best it can be. We'll also cover strategies for incorporating music, sound effects, and other elements into your podcast to enhance the listener experience.

Why Editing Is Important for Creating a Professional-Sounding Podcast

When it comes to producing a high-quality podcast, editing is a crucial step that should not be overlooked. Editing your podcast can help ensure that your content is polished, engaging, and professional-sounding. Here are some reasons why editing is so important for creating a successful podcast:

Removing Unwanted Content: During recording, there may be times when you stumble over your words or go off-topic. By editing these out, you can create a more concise and engaging podcast that holds your audience's attention.

Enhancing Audio Quality: Editing allows you to adjust levels and equalize the sound, which can help create a better listening experience for your audience. You can also remove background noise, adjust volumes, and enhance clarity.

Adding Sound Effects and Music: Editing your podcast also gives you the opportunity to add sound effects and music, which can help break up the content and make it more interesting and engaging for your listeners.

Providing a Consistent Listening Experience: Editing allows you to create a consistent listening experience for your audience by adjusting the sound quality, format, and pacing of your podcast. This helps to establish your podcast's brand and make it more recognizable.

By taking the time to edit your podcast, you can create a more engaging and professional-sounding product. However, it's important to keep in mind that the editing process can be time-consuming, so it's important to have a plan in place to streamline the process.

In the next chapters, we'll discuss tips and best practices for editing your podcast, including choosing the right software and tools, setting up an efficient workflow, and more.

Overview of common editing software and techniques

Editing is an essential step in creating a professional-sounding podcast. Even the best recordings can benefit from some editing to remove unwanted noise, mistakes, and awkward pauses. Fortunately, there are a variety of editing software options available that can help you to refine your podcast audio to a high standard.

Here's an overview of some of the most common podcast editing software options:

Audacity: Audacity is a free, open-source audio editing software that is easy to use and offers a range of features. It works on both Windows and Mac computers and has a simple interface that allows you to edit audio tracks, add effects, and more.

Adobe Audition: Adobe Audition is a more advanced audio editing software that offers a range of professional features, including multi-track editing, advanced noise reduction, and audio restoration tools. It is a paid software but is widely used by audio professionals.

GarageBand: GarageBand is a free audio editing software that is exclusive to Mac users. It is a great option for those new to audio editing and offers basic editing features such as trimming, volume adjustments, and the ability to add effects.

Hindenburg Journalist: Hindenburg Journalist is a paid audio editing software that is designed specifically for podcasters and journalists. It offers a range of features to enhance audio quality and make editing easier, such as automatic level adjustments and advanced EQ controls.

Once you've chosen your editing software, there are several techniques you can use to improve your podcast audio:

Cut out any unwanted noise or dead air: Use your editing software to remove any background noise, pops, or hisses, and cut out any pauses or silences in the audio.

Normalize the audio levels: Adjust the levels of the audio to make sure it is consistent throughout the podcast. You can use your editing software to increase or decrease the volume of individual tracks.

Add music and sound effects: Use music and sound effects to enhance your podcast and give it a professional feel. Make sure the music and effects are appropriately balanced with the spoken audio.

Edit out mistakes and stumbles: Listen through your recording and edit out any mistakes or stumbles to create a polished final product.

In conclusion, editing is an important step in creating a professional-sounding podcast. With the variety of editing software available, as well as the techniques available to improve your audio quality, it's possible to create a podcast that sounds polished and engaging.

Tips for editing your podcast to create a polished and engaging final product

Once you've recorded your podcast, the next step is to edit it to create a polished and engaging final product. Editing your podcast is important for creating a professional-sounding podcast that your audience will enjoy listening to. Here are some tips for editing your podcast:

Start with a plan: Before you start editing your podcast, make a plan for how you want the final product to sound. This will help you stay focused and ensure that you don't miss anything important.

Listen to the entire recording: Listen to the entire recording before you start editing. This will help you get a sense of the flow of the conversation and identify any parts that need to be cut or rearranged.

Cut out any unnecessary parts: Cut out any parts of the recording that are unnecessary or don't add value to the podcast. This could include long pauses, filler words, or parts of the conversation that don't fit with the overall theme of the podcast.

Use music and sound effects: Adding music and sound effects can help enhance the listening experience and make your podcast more engaging. However, be careful not to overdo it, as too many sound effects or a loud background track can be distracting.

Check audio levels: Make sure that the audio levels are consistent throughout the podcast. This means ensuring that the volume is not too high or too low and that the voices are clear and easy to understand.

Add transitions: Adding transitions between different parts of the podcast can help create a smoother listening experience. This could include fade-ins and fade-outs, music breaks, or sound effects.

Use a professional editing software: Using a professional editing software can help you create a high-quality podcast. There are many options available, including Audacity, GarageBand, and Adobe Audition.

Take breaks: Editing can be a tedious and time-consuming process. It's important to take breaks regularly to avoid burnout and maintain focus.

Get feedback: Once you've edited your podcast, listen to it again and get feedback from others. This can help you identify any areas that need improvement and ensure that your final product is the best it can be.

Editing your podcast is an important step in creating a professional-sounding podcast that your audience will enjoy listening to. By following these tips, you can create a polished and engaging final product that will help you build your audience and grow your podcast.

Strategies for incorporating music, sound effects, and other elements into your podcast

One of the keys to creating a successful podcast is making it engaging and interesting for your listeners. One way to do this is by incorporating music, sound effects, and other elements into your podcast. These elements can help set the tone for your show, create a sense of atmosphere, and make your content more memorable.

Here are some strategies for incorporating music, sound effects, and other elements into your podcast:

Choose the right music and sound effects: The music and sound effects you choose can greatly impact the mood and tone of your podcast. Make sure the music you select is appropriate for your content and enhances the message you are trying to convey. Similarly, sound effects can help create a sense of atmosphere and add impact to your content. Be sure to choose sounds that enhance your message, rather than detract from it.

Use music and sound effects sparingly: While incorporating music and sound effects can be a great way to enhance your content, it's important not to overdo it. Too much music and sound effects can be distracting and take away from the message you are trying to convey. Use them sparingly and purposefully to have the greatest impact.

Use music to bookend your show: Using a theme song or other music to introduce and close out your podcast can help create a sense of continuity and familiarity for your listeners. It can also help set the tone for your show and make it more memorable.

Incorporate interviews and other elements: Interviews and other elements, such as guest appearances or expert commentary, can also be great ways to enhance your content. By bringing in other voices and perspectives, you can make your podcast more interesting and engaging for your listeners.

Consider creating original music: If you have the talent and resources, creating original music for your podcast can be a great way to make it stand out and create a unique brand for your show. This can also help create a sense of continuity and familiarity for your listeners.

Incorporating music, sound effects, and other elements into your podcast can be a great way to enhance your content and make it more engaging and interesting for your listeners. By using these strategies, you can create a polished and professional final product that stands out in the crowded podcast landscape.

Editing your podcast is an essential part of the production process that can significantly impact its success. By taking the time to carefully edit your recordings, you can turn raw audio into a polished, engaging final product that will keep listeners coming back for more. In this chapter, we've covered the importance of editing, common editing software and techniques, and tips for creating a high-quality podcast. By incorporating these strategies into your editing process, you can produce a professional-sounding show that stands out in a crowded podcast landscape.

CHAPTER 15: IMPROVING AUDIO QUALITY

❖ How to Improve the Quality of Your Podcast Audio
❖ Tips for optimizing your recording environment and equipment to get the best possible sound
❖ Strategies for creating a professional-sounding podcast

While creating a podcast is an excellent way to share your thoughts and ideas with a wider audience, it's important to ensure that your audio quality is top-notch. Poor audio quality can make it difficult for your listeners to understand you and can even cause them to tune out altogether. In this chapter, we'll discuss how to improve the quality of your podcast audio, including techniques for reducing background noise, improving clarity, and enhancing overall sound quality.

How to Improve the Quality of Your Podcast Audio

The audio quality of your podcast can greatly impact the listening experience of your audience. Poor audio quality can lead to frustration and a lack of engagement, while high-quality audio can help to captivate and retain listeners. In this chapter, we'll explore various techniques and tools that you can use to improve the quality of your podcast audio.

Techniques for Reducing Background Noise
Background noise is a common issue that can reduce the quality of your podcast audio. Here are some techniques for reducing background noise:

Record in a quiet environment: Choose a space with minimal ambient noise, and avoid recording near appliances, fans, or other sources of noise.

Use a pop filter: A pop filter helps to reduce popping and plosive sounds that can be caused by the use of certain consonants.

Use noise reduction software: There are various noise reduction plugins available for audio editing software that can help to reduce background noise.

Techniques for Improving Clarity

Clarity is essential for ensuring that your audience can understand and engage with your content. Here are some techniques for improving clarity:

Speak clearly: Be sure to enunciate your words clearly, and avoid mumbling or speaking too quickly.

Use a high-quality microphone: A high-quality microphone can capture your voice with more clarity and detail than a low-quality one.

Use equalization: Equalization (EQ) is the process of adjusting the frequency balance of your audio. By making subtle EQ adjustments, you can enhance the clarity of your voice.

Techniques for Enhancing Overall Sound Quality

Improving the overall sound quality of your podcast can help to make it more engaging and professional. Here are some techniques for enhancing overall sound quality:

Use compression: Compression is a tool that can help to even out the volume of your audio. By compressing your audio, you can create a more consistent and polished sound.

Add reverb: Reverb can help to create a sense of space in your audio, which can make it sound more dynamic and engaging.

Use a limiter: A limiter is a tool that can prevent your audio from clipping, which can occur when your audio levels are too high.

By implementing these techniques and using the right tools, you can significantly improve the quality of your podcast audio.

Conclusion

Improving the quality of your podcast audio can help to make your content more engaging and professional. By using the right techniques and tools, you can reduce background noise, improve clarity, and enhance overall sound quality. Be sure to take the time to record in a quiet space, use a high-quality microphone, and experiment with EQ, compression, reverb, and limiters to achieve the best possible sound for your podcast.

Tips for optimizing your recording environment and equipment to get the best possible sound

In order to achieve high-quality sound for your podcast, it's important to optimize your recording environment and equipment. Here are some tips to help you get the best possible sound:

Choose a quiet recording location: The first step to improving your audio quality is to find a quiet location to record your podcast. Avoid areas with excessive ambient noise or distractions. If you're recording at home, choose a room that's furthest from any street noise, air conditioning or fans, and noisy appliances like refrigerators or washing machines.

Use acoustic treatment: Once you've found a quiet location, it's important to minimize any unwanted sound reflections or echo in the room. You can use acoustic treatment like sound-absorbing panels, blankets or carpets to reduce reverberation and improve clarity.

Position the microphone correctly: Positioning the microphone correctly is crucial to achieving good audio quality. Make sure to place the microphone at the optimal distance from your mouth to avoid distortion or popping sounds. You can use a pop filter to reduce plosives sounds caused by the letters "p" and "b".

Adjust recording levels: Check your recording levels and make sure they are set appropriately to avoid clipping or distortion. You should aim for a recording level that's not too quiet, which can introduce noise and require amplification in post-production, and not too loud which can introduce clipping.

Use high-quality equipment: Investing in high-quality recording equipment can make a big difference in the quality of your audio.

Consider purchasing a professional-grade microphone and headphones, as well as a high-quality audio interface or mixer.

Conduct sound checks: Before recording, conduct sound checks to ensure that your equipment is functioning properly, and your audio levels are optimized. You can also use software tools to analyze the sound quality and identify any issues with background noise or distortion.

Use noise reduction software: There are several noise reduction software options available to remove unwanted background noise from your recordings. However, it's important to use noise reduction tools sparingly as they can also remove desirable elements from your recording.

By optimizing your recording environment and equipment, you can significantly improve the sound quality of your podcast. Don't be afraid to experiment with different setups to find the optimal configuration that suits your needs and budget.

In the next chapter, we'll discuss techniques for reducing background noise, improving clarity, and enhancing overall sound quality during the editing process.

Strategies for troubleshooting common audio issues and improving your podcast's overall sound quality

No matter how well you prepare or how advanced your equipment is, audio issues can still happen when recording a podcast. These can range from background noise and echo to distortion and low volume. The good news is that many of these issues can be addressed with some troubleshooting techniques and sound quality improvements. In this chapter, we'll discuss some strategies for troubleshooting common audio issues and improving your podcast's overall sound quality.

Identify the source of the problem

The first step in troubleshooting audio issues is to identify the source of the problem. Is it an issue with your recording environment, your equipment, or your recording software? Is it a problem with your mic, your headphones, or your audio interface? Once you've identified the source of the problem, you can take steps to address it.

Reduce background noise

Background noise is one of the most common audio issues that podcasters face. Some ways to reduce background noise include recording in a quiet environment, using a noise gate in your recording software, and positioning your mic closer to your mouth to reduce the amount of ambient noise it picks up.

Eliminate echo and reverb

Echo and reverb can be caused by recording in a large, open space with hard surfaces that reflect sound. To eliminate echo and reverb, consider recording in a smaller, more acoustically treated space, or using acoustic panels or blankets to absorb sound reflections.

Address distortion

Distortion can occur when your audio levels are too high and your recording equipment can't handle the signal. To address distortion, try reducing the gain on your mic or audio interface, or moving further away from the mic to reduce the level.

Enhance overall sound quality

There are several ways to enhance the overall sound quality of your podcast. One of the most effective ways is to use a high-quality microphone and audio interface. Other strategies include using equalization to balance the frequency response of your audio, using compression to even out the levels of your audio, and using a limiter to prevent audio peaks from clipping.

Test and refine

Once you've addressed any audio issues and made sound quality improvements, it's important to test and refine your recording setup to make sure you're getting the best possible sound. This may involve experimenting with mic placement, adjusting your recording environment, or tweaking your recording software settings.

By taking these steps to troubleshoot common audio issues and improve your podcast's overall sound quality, you can create a professional-sounding podcast that engages and entertains your audience.

In conclusion, while audio issues can be frustrating, there are many strategies for addressing them and improving your podcast's sound quality. By taking the time to identify the source of the problem, reduce background noise, eliminate echo and reverb, address distortion, enhance overall sound quality, and test and refine your setup, you can create a podcast with high-quality audio that your audience will love to listen to.

By implementing the tips and strategies outlined in this chapter, you'll be well on your way to producing high-quality audio for your podcast. Remember, audio quality is an essential component of creating a professional-sounding podcast, and taking the time to optimize your recording environment and equipment can make a significant difference in the overall quality of your final product. With a little bit of effort and some careful attention to detail, you can create an engaging and enjoyable podcast that your listeners will love.

Strategies for creating a professional-sounding podcast

Creating a professional-sounding podcast involves more than just having the right equipment and software. You also need to focus on the content and delivery of your podcast to keep your audience engaged and interested. Here are some strategies for creating a professional-sounding podcast:

Script your podcast: While some podcasters may prefer to speak off-the-cuff, having a script can help you stay on track and ensure that you cover all the necessary points. A script can also help you maintain a consistent tone and pace throughout your podcast.

Pay attention to pacing: The pace of your podcast can have a big impact on how engaged your audience is. If you speak too quickly, your audience may struggle to keep up, but if you speak too slowly, they may lose interest. Find a pace that feels natural for you, and consider adding pauses for emphasis or to give your listeners time to process what you've just said.

Focus on your delivery: Your tone of voice and delivery style can have a big impact on how your audience perceives your podcast. Speak clearly and confidently, and try to vary your tone to keep things interesting. Don't be afraid to inject some personality into your delivery, whether it's through humor, storytelling, or other techniques.

Create engaging content: To keep your audience coming back for more, you need to create content that resonates with them. Think about your target audience and what they're interested in, and tailor your content accordingly. Consider interviewing experts in your field, sharing personal stories, or presenting interesting facts and statistics to keep things engaging.

Keep things concise: While there's no set length for a podcast, it's important to keep your episodes concise and focused. Try to stay on topic and avoid rambling, and consider breaking longer episodes into shorter segments or series to make them more digestible for your audience.

By following these strategies, you can create a professional-sounding podcast that keeps your audience engaged and coming back for more. Remember to experiment and try new things to see what works best for you and your audience.

CHAPTER 16: CREATING A PROFESSIONAL SOUNDING PODCAST

❖ Best practices for creating a professional-sounding podcast, including techniques for scripting, pacing, and delivery
❖ Tips for creating engaging and compelling content that resonates with your audience
❖ Strategies for building a strong brand and following for your podcast
❖ Examples of successful podcasts with high-quality audio and professional-sounding content

Best practices for creating a professional-sounding podcast, including techniques for scripting, pacing, and delivery

Creating a successful podcast takes more than just good equipment and technical know-how. To truly stand out and capture the attention of listeners, it's important to create a professional-sounding podcast with high-quality content and engaging delivery. In this chapter, we'll explore some best practices for creating a professional-sounding podcast, including techniques for scripting, pacing, and delivery.

Scripting Your Podcast
One of the most important steps in creating a professional-sounding podcast is to have a well-written and thought-out script. This helps to ensure that your content is organized and flows smoothly, while also allowing you to control the pace and delivery of your message. When writing your script, consider the following:

Clearly define the topic and purpose of your podcast.
Use language that is accessible and easy to understand for your target audience.

Organize your content in a logical and coherent way, using headings, bullet points, and other formatting techniques.

Incorporate engaging and compelling stories, examples, and analogies to help illustrate your points.

Include clear and concise calls-to-action that encourage your listeners to engage with your content and share it with others.

Pacing Your Podcast

Another important aspect of creating a professional-sounding podcast is pacing. You want to keep your listeners engaged and interested throughout the entire episode, which requires a careful balance of energy and flow. Some tips for pacing your podcast include:

Vary your tone and energy level to keep your listeners engaged and interested.

Use pauses and breaks strategically to give your listeners time to process information and reflect on what you've said.

Avoid speaking too quickly or too slowly, as both can make it difficult for your listeners to follow along.

Incorporate music or other audio elements to help break up the pacing and add variety to your podcast.

Delivering Your Podcast

Finally, delivering your podcast with confidence and authenticity is essential for creating a professional-sounding product. You want to come across as knowledgeable, engaging, and approachable, while also staying true to your own voice and style. Some tips for delivering your podcast include:

Practice your delivery ahead of time, rehearsing your script and testing your pacing and tone.

Speak clearly and enunciate your words, so that your listeners can easily follow along.

Use intonation and inflection to add variety and interest to your delivery.

Consider incorporating humor or personal anecdotes to help connect with your listeners on a more personal level.

In conclusion, creating a professional-sounding podcast requires attention to detail, careful planning, and a commitment to quality content and delivery. By following these best practices for scripting, pacing, and delivering your podcast, you can create a product that engages and captivates your listeners, while also building your brand and reputation in the podcasting world.

Tips for Creating Engaging and Compelling Content

Creating engaging and compelling content is essential to the success of any podcast. The quality of your content can make or break your podcast, so it's important to put a lot of thought and effort into creating content that resonates with your audience. In this chapter, we'll go over some tips for creating content that keeps your listeners engaged and coming back for more.

Define Your Target Audience
Before you start creating content, it's important to know who your target audience is. Knowing your audience will help you create content that speaks to their needs and interests. Consider factors such as age, gender, interests, and education level when defining your target audience.

Be Authentic and Passionate
One of the key factors that set successful podcasts apart from the rest is the passion and authenticity of the hosts. Be yourself, and let your true personality shine through. Authenticity is what draws people in and keeps them coming back for more.

Develop a Strong Hook
You need to grab your listener's attention right from the start, and a strong hook is the perfect way to do this. The first few seconds of your podcast are critical, so make sure you have a powerful and attention-grabbing opening.

Use Storytelling Techniques

People love stories, and incorporating storytelling into your podcast is a great way to keep your listeners engaged. Use anecdotes and personal experiences to illustrate your points and connect with your audience.

Keep Your Content Fresh

Don't get stuck in a rut by discussing the same topics over and over again. Keep your content fresh by exploring new angles and bringing in guests with different perspectives. Consider conducting interviews, having guest hosts, or switching up the format of your podcast to keep things interesting.

Use Clear and Concise Language

Speak in a clear and concise manner to help your listeners understand your content. Avoid using jargon or technical terms unless it's absolutely necessary, and be mindful of your pace and tone to help convey your message effectively.

Encourage Interaction

Encourage your listeners to interact with your podcast by asking for feedback or hosting Q&A sessions. This can help you build a stronger relationship with your audience and provide valuable insights into what your listeners want to hear.

Stick to a Schedule

Consistency is key in podcasting, so make sure you're sticking to a regular schedule. This can help build anticipation and keep your listeners engaged.

Incorporating these tips into your podcasting strategy can help you create content that resonates with your audience and keeps them coming back for more.

In conclusion, creating engaging and compelling content is critical to the success of your podcast. By defining your target audience, being authentic and passionate, developing a strong hook, using storytelling techniques, keeping your content fresh, using clear and concise language, encouraging interaction, and sticking to a regular schedule, you can create a podcast that keeps your listeners engaged and coming back for more.

Conclusion:

In conclusion, audio quality is a critical factor in the success of your podcast. By following the tips and strategies outlined in this chapter, you can improve the clarity, crispness, and overall sound quality of your podcast. From optimizing your recording environment and equipment to troubleshooting common audio issues, there are many steps you can take to enhance the listening experience of your audience. With high-quality audio, your podcast will stand out in a crowded marketplace and attract a growing and engaged audience.

CHAPTER 17: CHOOSING A PODCAST HOSTING PLATFORM

❖ Overview of popular podcast hosting platforms, including their features, pricing, and pros and cons
❖ Strategies for choosing the right hosting platform for your needs and budget
❖ Best practices for setting up your hosting account and uploading your podcast episodes
❖ Tips for optimizing your podcast hosting account for better performance and visibility

If you want to share your podcast with the world, you need a hosting platform to store and distribute your audio files. But with so many options available, it can be overwhelming to choose the right platform for your needs. In this chapter, we'll explore some of the most popular podcast hosting platforms, their features, pricing, and pros and cons, and provide tips for optimizing your account for better performance and visibility.

Introduction:
As a podcaster, finding the right hosting platform is crucial for the success of your show. It's where you'll store your episodes, distribute them to various podcast directories, and analyze your audience data. With so many options to choose from, it can be challenging to select the right platform for your needs. That's why in this chapter, we'll give you an overview of the most popular podcast hosting platforms and share strategies for choosing the right one for your show.

Overview of popular podcast hosting platforms, including their features, pricing, and pros and cons

If you want to share your podcast with the world, you'll need to use a podcast hosting platform. These platforms store and distribute your podcast episodes to various podcast directories such as Apple Podcasts, Spotify, and Google Podcasts. There are numerous hosting platforms available, each with their own features, pricing, and pros and cons. In this chapter, we'll provide an overview of some of the most popular podcast hosting platforms to help you choose the best one for your needs.

Overview of Popular Podcast Hosting Platforms
Buzzsprout - Buzzsprout is a popular podcast hosting platform that offers a simple, user-friendly interface. It offers several pricing plans starting from free with limited features, up to $24/month for advanced features. Some of the features include podcast statistics, embeddable players, and support for multiple users.

Libsyn - Libsyn has been around since 2004 and is one of the oldest and most popular podcast hosting platforms. It offers various pricing plans starting at $5/month, up to $150/month for more advanced features. Some of the features include monetization options, custom mobile apps, and detailed analytics.

Transistor - Transistor offers a wide range of features that cater to podcasters of all levels. It offers various pricing plans starting at $19/month, up to $99/month for advanced features. Some of the features include private podcasting, podcast analytics, and automatic episode transcripts.

Captivate - Captivate offers an all-in-one podcast hosting and analytics platform that provides a range of useful features for podcasters. It offers various pricing plans starting at $19/month, up to $99/month for more advanced features. Some of the features include podcast analytics, custom domains, and integrations with popular marketing tools.

Podbean - Podbean is a user-friendly podcast hosting platform that offers a range of features to help podcasters grow their audience. It offers various pricing plans starting at $9/month, up to $99/month for more advanced features. Some of the features include podcast statistics, custom domains, and monetization options.

Blubrry - Blubrry offers a range of hosting plans that cater to podcasters of all levels. It offers various pricing plans starting at $12/month, up to $80/month for more advanced features. Some of the features include podcast statistics, WordPress integration, and advertising opportunities.

Conclusion
Choosing the right podcast hosting platform is an important decision that can affect the success of your podcast. By considering the features, pricing, and pros and cons of each hosting platform, you can find the one that best suits your needs. Ultimately, the most important factor to consider is whether the platform can help you reach your target audience and grow your podcast.

Strategies for choosing the right hosting platform for your needs and budget
When it comes to launching a podcast, choosing the right hosting platform is essential. The hosting platform you choose will be responsible for hosting and distributing your podcast to various podcast directories, as well as providing you with the tools you need to manage your episodes, track your audience metrics, and monetize your podcast. Here are some strategies for choosing the right hosting platform for your needs and budget.

Consider your budget: There are many podcast hosting platforms available, and their prices can vary significantly. Some platforms offer free plans, while others require a monthly or annual subscription fee. Think about your budget and what you can afford before you start your search. Keep in mind that the price of hosting may increase as your podcast grows.

Look for a platform that offers the features you need: Every podcast is unique, and the hosting platform you choose should provide you with the features you need to create and distribute your podcast successfully. Consider features such as storage space, analytics tools, monetization options, and support for multiple shows or users.

Check out reviews and ratings: Look for reviews and ratings from other podcasters to get an idea of the platform's reliability, user-friendliness, and overall quality. You can find reviews on websites such as Podchaser, as well as on social media platforms.

Evaluate the platform's customer support: Make sure the hosting platform you choose offers reliable and responsive customer support. If you encounter technical issues, you want to be sure you can get help quickly and efficiently.

Consider the platform's distribution channels: Some podcast hosting platforms offer better distribution channels than others. Consider which directories the platform supports, and how easy it is to distribute your podcast to those directories. Some platforms may also offer additional features, such as social media promotion or advertising options.

Test the platform's user interface: Before you commit to a hosting platform, take the time to test its user interface. Look for a platform that is easy to use and navigate, and that provides you with the tools you need to manage your podcast effectively.

By considering these strategies, you can choose a podcast hosting platform that meets your needs and fits your budget.

In conclusion, selecting the right podcast hosting platform is critical to the success of your podcast. You need a platform that provides you with the features and tools you need to create, distribute, and manage your podcast effectively. By following the strategies outlined above, you can find a hosting platform that meets your needs and helps you achieve your podcasting goals.

Best practices for setting up your hosting account and uploading your podcast episodes

Once you've chosen your podcast hosting platform, it's time to set up your account and start uploading your podcast episodes. Here are some best practices to keep in mind:

Create a branded account: Use your podcast name or brand name when creating your hosting account. This will help listeners find your podcast more easily when searching for it on the platform.

Choose the right plan: Depending on your needs and budget, you may want to choose a free plan or a paid plan that offers additional features such as more storage space or advanced analytics. Consider how many episodes you plan to upload per month and how large they are in file size.

Optimize your episode titles and descriptions: Use descriptive titles and descriptions for each episode that include relevant keywords and phrases. This will help listeners find your podcast when searching for topics related to your episodes.

Create episode artwork: Your podcast hosting platform will likely require you to upload episode artwork along with your audio file. Make sure your artwork is consistent with your podcast branding and is eye-catching to attract listeners.

Upload your audio file: Make sure your audio file is in the correct format and meets the platform's file size requirements. Most platforms support the common audio formats like MP3 and WAV.

Add metadata and tags: Along with your episode titles and descriptions, you'll want to add metadata such as episode numbers, release dates, and guest names. You can also add tags that describe the topic or theme of the episode. This will help listeners find your podcast when searching for specific topics or guests.

Schedule your episodes: Most hosting platforms allow you to schedule your episodes to be released at a specific time and date. This can help you maintain a consistent publishing schedule and build anticipation for your episodes.

Test your episodes: Before you publish your episodes, make sure to test them to ensure they play correctly and sound good. Listen to them on different devices and in different environments to catch any issues or audio glitches.

By following these best practices, you can ensure a smooth and professional upload process for your podcast episodes on your chosen hosting platform.

Tips for optimizing your podcast hosting account for better performance and visibility

When it comes to podcast hosting, there are a few key strategies you can use to optimize your account for better performance and visibility. Here are some tips for using two popular hosting platforms, Red Circle and Buzzsprout:

Red Circle
1. Customize your show settings
Make sure to customize your show settings in Red Circle to optimize for search engine optimization (SEO) and discovery. This includes adding relevant keywords to your show description and title, selecting appropriate categories and subcategories, and creating a unique cover art.

2. Set up automatic social media sharing
Red Circle offers an automatic social media sharing feature that allows you to share new episodes on your social media profiles as soon as they go live. This can help increase your visibility and attract new listeners.

3. Use dynamic ad insertion

Red Circle offers dynamic ad insertion, which allows you to insert targeted ads into your podcast episodes. This can help you monetize your podcast and improve your revenue.

Buzzsprout

1. Optimize your episode titles and descriptions

Make sure to optimize your episode titles and descriptions for SEO by including relevant keywords and phrases. This can help your episodes show up in search results and increase your visibility.

2. Use chapter markers

Buzzsprout allows you to add chapter markers to your episodes, which can help listeners navigate to specific sections of your podcast. This can make your podcast more user-friendly and increase engagement.

3. Leverage Buzzsprout's promotional tools

Buzzsprout offers a range of promotional tools, such as the ability to create an audiogram to share on social media, to help you promote your podcast and reach a wider audience.

By following these tips, you can optimize your podcast hosting account for better performance and visibility on platforms like Red Circle and Buzzsprout.

Conclusion

Optimizing your podcast hosting account is an important part of building and growing your podcast audience. By customizing your show settings, setting up automatic social media sharing, using dynamic ad insertion, optimizing your episode titles and descriptions, using chapter markers, and leveraging promotional tools, you can improve the performance and visibility of your podcast. Be sure to explore the features of your hosting platform and try out different strategies to find what works best for your podcast.

Choosing the right podcast hosting platform is an important decision for any podcaster. By understanding the features, pricing, and pros and cons of each platform, you can make an informed decision that suits your needs and budget. Remember to consider factors such as storage capacity, distribution options, analytics, and support when choosing a platform. With the right hosting provider and a solid strategy, you can take your podcast to the next level and reach a wider audience.

CHAPTER 18: SETTING UP YOUR PODCAST RSS FEED

❖ What is an RSS feed and why is it important for podcasting?
❖ How to set up your podcast RSS feed using your hosting platform
❖ Strategies for optimizing your RSS feed for better performance and visibility
❖ Best practices for testing and validating your RSS feed to ensure it's working correctly

If you're new to the world of podcasting, you may have heard the term "RSS feed" thrown around without really understanding what it means. In short, an RSS (Really Simple Syndication) feed is a way for listeners to subscribe to your podcast and receive new episodes automatically as they're released. But why is an RSS feed so important for podcasting? In this chapter, we'll explore the basics of RSS feeds and why they're essential for podcast distribution. We'll also provide tips for setting up and optimizing your RSS feed to ensure your podcast is easily discoverable and accessible to your audience.

What is an RSS feed and why is it important for podcasting?

When it comes to podcasting, there's one important term you need to know: RSS feed. An RSS (Really Simple Syndication) feed is a file that contains your podcast's metadata and audio content. It is this file that allows your listeners to access and subscribe to your podcast on various platforms like Apple Podcasts, Spotify, Google Podcasts, and more.

In essence, an RSS feed is what powers your podcast's distribution across different listening platforms. Without an RSS feed, your podcast would not be able to reach your intended audience.

So, why is an RSS feed so important for podcasting? Here are a few key reasons:

Distribution: As mentioned, an RSS feed is what allows your podcast to be distributed to various listening platforms. When you upload a new episode to your hosting platform and update your RSS feed, it triggers a signal to these platforms, notifying them that new content is available. This is how your listeners can access your latest episodes and subscribe to your podcast.

Discoverability: Having an RSS feed also makes your podcast more discoverable. Most podcast directories like Apple Podcasts and Spotify use RSS feeds to populate their directories. If your podcast is not in these directories, it will be harder for listeners to find and subscribe to your show.

Customization: Another advantage of having an RSS feed is that it allows you to customize the way your podcast appears on different platforms. You can add show notes, episode descriptions, and artwork to your RSS feed, which will then be displayed on different listening platforms.

Overall, an RSS feed is a crucial component of your podcast's distribution and discovery. Without it, your show will not be available on various listening platforms, and your audience will be limited.

In the next chapter, we'll explore how to create an RSS feed for your podcast and make sure it's set up correctly.

How to set up your podcast RSS feed using your hosting platform

One of the most important aspects of podcasting is having an RSS feed. An RSS feed is a file that contains information about your podcast, such as the title, description, and episode list, that allows podcast directories to display and distribute your content. Without an RSS feed, your podcast cannot be distributed to popular podcast directories such as Apple Podcasts, Spotify, and Google Podcasts.

The good news is that if you're using a podcast hosting platform, setting up your RSS feed is typically a simple process. Here's how to set up your podcast RSS feed using your hosting platform:

Sign up for a podcast hosting platform that provides an RSS feed, such as Buzzsprout, Libsyn, or Podbean.

Create your podcast, including a title, description, and cover art.

Upload your podcast episodes to your hosting platform.

Check that your podcast information and episodes are correctly displayed on your hosting platform.

Locate your podcast's RSS feed URL on your hosting platform. This will be the URL that podcast directories will use to access your podcast.

Submit your podcast's RSS feed to popular podcast directories, such as Apple Podcasts, Spotify, and Google Podcasts, to make your podcast available to listeners.

Regularly update your RSS feed with new episodes to keep your podcast current and fresh.

By setting up your podcast RSS feed using your hosting platform, you'll have an efficient and reliable way to distribute your podcast to a wide audience. Additionally, hosting platforms typically provide tools to help you track your podcast's performance, including download statistics and audience demographics, so you can continue to refine your podcast and grow your listener base.

In conclusion, setting up your podcast RSS feed is a critical step in making your podcast available to listeners around the world. With the right hosting platform and by following these steps, you can create and manage a professional-looking RSS feed that allows you to distribute your podcast to a broad audience.

Strategies for optimizing your RSS feed for better performance and visibility

One of the most important aspects of your podcast is your RSS feed, which allows your listeners to subscribe to your show and receive updates when new episodes are released. To make sure your podcast is easily discoverable and accessible, it's essential to optimize your RSS feed for better performance and visibility. Here are some strategies for doing just that:

Use a descriptive title and description: Your podcast title and description should be clear and descriptive, giving listeners a good idea of what your show is about. This will help them find your podcast when searching for topics related to your show.

Include relevant keywords: Incorporate relevant keywords in your podcast title, description, and episode titles. This will help your show rank higher in search results, making it easier for listeners to find your podcast.

Use high-quality artwork: Your podcast artwork is the first thing listeners see when they discover your show. Make sure it's eye-catching, high-quality, and clearly represents your podcast.

Keep your RSS feed updated: It's essential to keep your RSS feed updated with new episodes and relevant information. This ensures that your listeners always have access to your latest content.

Optimize your episode titles: Your episode titles should be descriptive, catchy, and include relevant keywords. This will help your episodes show up in search results and attract new listeners.

Include show notes: Show notes provide additional information about your podcast episodes, including guest bios, resources, and links.

This can help attract new listeners and provide value to your current audience.

Submit your RSS feed to directories: Submitting your RSS feed to popular podcast directories such as Apple Podcasts, Spotify, and Google Podcasts can help increase your show's visibility and attract new listeners.

Monitor your RSS feed performance: Keep an eye on your RSS feed performance and analytics to see what's working and what's not. This can help you make data-driven decisions to improve your podcast's performance and reach.

By implementing these strategies, you can optimize your podcast's RSS feed for better performance and visibility, making it easier for new listeners to discover and subscribe to your show.

Best practices for testing and validating your RSS feed to ensure it's working correctly

Creating and setting up your podcast RSS feed is an important step in the podcasting process, but it's not enough to just set it up and forget about it. It's essential to test and validate your RSS feed to make sure it's working correctly, and that your podcast is being delivered to listeners through their favorite podcast players.

Here are some best practices for testing and validating your podcast RSS feed:

Use a feed validator: There are several free feed validators available online that can help you check your RSS feed for errors and ensure it meets industry standards. Some popular validators include FeedValidator.org and Podbase Validator. Simply enter your RSS feed URL and the validator will provide a report of any errors or issues.

Test your RSS feed on multiple podcast players: It's important to test your RSS feed on multiple podcast players to ensure that it's working correctly and your podcast is accessible to listeners on different platforms. Some popular podcast players to test on include Apple Podcasts, Spotify, Google Podcasts, and Stitcher.

Check for consistent updates: Your RSS feed should be updated every time you publish a new episode. Check your feed regularly to make sure that new episodes are being added and published consistently. Inconsistent updates can result in your podcast not showing up in podcast player directories or not being accessible to listeners.

Monitor your download and subscription numbers: Keep an eye on your download and subscription numbers to make sure that they're increasing over time. A sudden drop in numbers could indicate an issue with your RSS feed or podcast hosting platform.

Double-check your episode information: Make sure that your episode information, including titles, descriptions, and media files, are all accurate and properly linked in your RSS feed. Incorrect or missing information can cause issues with your podcast's delivery to listeners.

Consider hiring a professional: If you're not tech-savvy or don't have the time to test and validate your RSS feed, consider hiring a professional to help. There are many podcast consultants and service providers who specialize in podcasting and can help ensure your RSS feed is working correctly.

Testing and validating your podcast RSS feed is a crucial step in the podcasting process. By following these best practices, you can ensure that your podcast is accessible to listeners and that you're delivering a high-quality listening experience.

An RSS feed is a crucial component of podcasting. It's what allows your listeners to subscribe to your podcast and receive new episodes automatically. By setting up and optimizing your RSS feed, you can ensure that your podcast is easily discoverable and accessible to your audience. Whether you're new to podcasting or you've been doing it for a while, it's important to understand the basics of RSS feeds and how to use them effectively. With the strategies and tips provided in this chapter, you'll be well on your way to creating a successful and sustainable podcast.

CHAPTER 19: SUBMITTING YOUR PODCAST TO DIRECTORIES

❖ Overview of popular podcast directories, including Apple Podcasts, Google Podcasts, and Spotify
❖ Submitting Your Podcast to Directories and Optimizing Your Listing
❖ Best practices for managing your podcast listings and updating them as needed
❖ Strategies for leveraging podcast directories to build your audience and grow your podcast

If you want your podcast to reach a wider audience, submitting it to popular podcast directories like Apple Podcasts, Google Podcasts, and Spotify is essential. But simply submitting your podcast isn't enough. You also need to optimize your listing to make it more discoverable and appealing to potential listeners. In this chapter, we'll provide an overview of popular podcast directories, show you how to submit your podcast and optimize your listing, and offer tips for leveraging directories to grow your audience.

Overview of popular podcast directories, including Apple Podcasts, Google Podcasts, and Spotify

If you want to make sure that your podcast reaches the widest possible audience, it's essential to have it listed on popular podcast directories. These directories are websites and apps that people use to discover, stream, and download podcasts.

Here are some of the most popular podcast directories that you should consider listing your podcast on:

Apple Podcasts: This is the most popular podcast directory, with over a billion active users. It's exclusive to Apple devices and has a massive library of podcasts across all genres.

Google Podcasts: This directory is available on both Android and iOS devices and is integrated with the Google Assistant. It has a simple interface that's easy to navigate and discover new podcasts.

Spotify: This music streaming service has rapidly become one of the most popular podcast directories in recent years. It has over 300 million active users and a large selection of podcasts across various categories.

Stitcher: This directory has been around for over a decade and has an extensive collection of over 100,000 podcasts across all genres. It's available on both iOS and Android devices and has a user-friendly interface.

TuneIn: This directory is available on both iOS and Android devices and has a massive selection of over 100,000 podcasts. It also has a live radio feature, which makes it an excellent option for news and sports podcasts.

Other popular podcast directories include iHeartRadio, Overcast, and Pocket Casts. Each directory has its own unique features, so it's worth considering listing your podcast on multiple platforms to reach the widest possible audience.

It's worth noting that some directories require an application process, while others will automatically add your podcast based on your RSS feed. Make sure you follow the submission guidelines for each directory to ensure your podcast is listed correctly.

In the next few chapters, we'll cover the steps you need to take to get your podcast listed on these directories, starting with Apple Podcasts.

Submitting Your Podcast to Directories and Optimizing Your Listing

Once you have recorded and edited your podcast, the next step is to share it with the world. One of the best ways to do this is by submitting your podcast to directories like Apple Podcasts, Google Podcasts, and Spotify. These directories make it easy for listeners to find and subscribe to your podcast, and can help you reach a wider audience. In this chapter, we'll go over how to submit your podcast to directories and optimize your listing for better visibility and discoverability starting with Apple Podcasts.

Overview of Popular Podcast Directories

There are several popular podcast directories where you can submit your podcast, including:

Apple Podcasts: The largest and most popular podcast directory in the world, with over one million shows and over 30 million episodes available for download.

Google Podcasts: Google's podcast directory, available on Android devices and via Google Assistant.

Spotify: The largest music streaming service in the world, which has recently expanded into the podcasting space.

Stitcher: A popular podcast directory and app, which offers both free and premium content.

How to Submit Your Podcast to Directories

Each podcast directory has its own submission process, but in general, you will need to follow these steps:

Create an account: Most directories will require you to create an account before you can submit your podcast.

Prepare your podcast information: You will need to provide information about your podcast, including its title, description, category, and cover art.

Verify ownership of your podcast: Some directories, like Apple Podcasts, require you to verify ownership of your podcast before it can be listed.

Submit your podcast: Once you have completed the above steps, you can submit your podcast to the directory.

Optimizing Your Listing

Once your podcast is listed in a directory, you will want to optimize your listing to increase visibility and discoverability. Here are some tips for optimizing your listing in Apple Podcasts:

Choose the right categories: Apple Podcasts allows you to choose up to three categories for your podcast. Be sure to choose categories that accurately reflect the content of your show, as this will help listeners find your podcast when searching for specific topics.

Write a compelling description: Your podcast description should be clear, concise, and engaging. It should give listeners an idea of what your show is about and why they should listen.

Use high-quality cover art: Your cover art is often the first thing listeners will see when browsing through podcasts. Make sure it is eye-catching and high-quality.

Encourage reviews and ratings: Positive reviews and ratings can help your podcast rank higher in search results. Encourage your listeners to leave a review or rating on Apple Podcasts.

Promote your podcast: Once your podcast is listed in Apple Podcasts, promote it on social media and other channels to increase its visibility.

Conclusion

Submitting your podcast to directories like Apple Podcasts, Google Podcasts, and Spotify can help you reach a wider audience and increase the visibility of your show. By following the steps outlined in this chapter and optimizing your listing for better discoverability, you can increase your chances of success and grow your podcast over time.

Best practices for managing your podcast listings and updating them as needed

Once you've submitted your podcast to directories like Apple Podcasts, Google Podcasts, and Spotify, it's important to keep your listings up-to-date and optimized for maximum visibility and discoverability. Here are some best practices for managing your podcast listings and updating them as needed:

Keep your podcast title and description up-to-date: Your podcast title and description are the first things potential listeners will see when browsing the directory, so it's important to make sure they accurately reflect your show's content and tone. Consider updating them periodically to keep them fresh and relevant.

Add or update cover art: Your podcast's cover art is another important element of your listing, as it can help your show stand out and attract potential listeners. Make sure your cover art is high-quality and visually appealing, and consider updating it periodically to keep it fresh.

Update your episode descriptions: Your episode descriptions are a key tool for attracting new listeners and providing context for your existing audience. Make sure your episode descriptions are clear and engaging, and include relevant keywords to help your episodes appear in search results.

Respond to reviews and comments: Engaging with your audience is an important part of building a loyal following for your podcast. Take the time to respond to reviews and comments on your listings, and thank your listeners for their support.

Monitor your analytics: Most podcast directories offer analytics tools that can help you track your show's performance and audience engagement. Use these tools to monitor your downloads, listener demographics, and other metrics, and adjust your strategy as needed to optimize your results.

Update your links: If you move your podcast to a new hosting platform or change your website URL, it's important to update the links in your directory listings to avoid broken links and ensure a seamless listening experience for your audience.

By following these best practices for managing your podcast listings and updating them as needed, you can help ensure that your show reaches the widest possible audience and continues to grow over time.

Strategies for leveraging podcast directories to build your audience and grow your podcast

Submitting your podcast to popular directories like Apple Podcasts, Google Podcasts, and Spotify is just the first step in building an audience for your show. To truly leverage these platforms, you need to be strategic about how you present and promote your podcast. In this chapter, we'll explore some effective strategies for making the most of podcast directories to grow your audience and increase your reach.

Optimize Your Listing

Your podcast listing is your first impression on potential listeners, so it's important to make it count. Take the time to craft an engaging podcast description, choose an eye-catching cover art, and select appropriate categories and tags for your show. You want your listing to be informative, visually appealing, and easy to find through search.

Encourage Ratings and Reviews

Ratings and reviews are critical social proof that can help attract new listeners to your show. Encourage your existing audience to leave honest reviews and ratings on your podcast listing, and be sure to respond to any feedback you receive. Not only will this help build credibility for your show, but it will also give you valuable insights into what your listeners like and what they want more of.

Engage with Other Podcasters

Networking with other podcasters can help you tap into new audiences and gain valuable insights into what works in the podcasting world. Connect with other podcasters through social media, industry events, and online communities, and be sure to promote each other's shows on your respective platforms. Collaborating with other podcasters on guest interviews or cross-promotions can also help you tap into new audiences and expand your reach.

Leverage Paid Advertising

While many podcasters rely on organic growth through word of mouth and social media, paid advertising can also be a highly effective way to reach new listeners. Many podcast directories, including Apple Podcasts, offer advertising options that allow you to target specific demographics and reach new audiences. Experiment with different ad formats and messaging to find what resonates with your target audience.

Monitor Your Analytics

Finally, it's important to regularly monitor your analytics to track your podcast's performance and identify areas for improvement. Podcast directories like Apple Podcasts and Spotify offer basic analytics that can give you insight into your show's downloads, listener demographics, and more. You can also use third-party analytics tools to get more detailed information about your listeners and their behavior. Use this information to inform your content and marketing strategies and continually optimize your approach.

By following these strategies, you can make the most of podcast directories to build your audience and grow your show. Remember, the key to success in podcasting is to continually experiment, iterate, and improve. Keep testing new strategies and tweaking your approach until you find what works best for your show and your audience.

Conclusion:

Podcast directories are powerful tools for building your audience and growing your podcast. By optimizing your listing, encouraging ratings and reviews, engaging with other podcasters, leveraging paid advertising, and monitoring your analytics, you can make the most of these platforms and reach new listeners. Remember, the key to success in podcasting is to experiment, iterate, and continually improve. Keep testing new strategies and adapting your approach to meet the needs and preferences of your audience. With persistence, hard work, and a bit of creativity, you can build a loyal following and achieve success in the exciting and dynamic world of podcasting.

In conclusion, podcast directories are a powerful tool for building your audience and expanding the reach of your podcast. By submitting your podcast to popular directories and optimizing your listing, you can make it easier for people to find and discover your content. But submitting your podcast is just the first step. To truly leverage podcast directories, you need to actively promote your podcast and engage with your listeners. By using the strategies outlined in this chapter, you can take your podcast to the next level and reach new heights of success.

CHAPTER 20: CREATING PODCAST SHOW NOTES

❖ What are podcast show notes and why are they important for your podcast?
❖ Strategies for creating effective and engaging show notes that provide value to your audience
❖ Tips for optimizing your show notes for better SEO and searchability
❖ Best Practices for Formatting and Structuring Your Show Notes

In this chapter, we'll explore the importance of podcast show notes and provide tips on how to create effective and engaging show notes for your audience. Show notes are an essential element of your podcast that provide additional information and context about your episodes, as well as help listeners find and discover your content through search engines and podcast directories. Effective show notes can also help build your credibility, enhance your brand image, and keep your audience engaged beyond your podcast episodes.

Let's dive into the strategies and best practices for creating compelling and well-formatted show notes.

What are podcast show notes and why are they important for your podcast

Podcast show notes are a written summary or transcript of each episode of a podcast. They are posted on the podcast's website, along with the audio file, and provide listeners with additional information about the episode's content. Show notes can include a brief summary of the episode's topic, guest information, links to relevant resources, and timestamps for specific segments within the episode.

Podcast show notes are important for several reasons. First, they provide a way for listeners to quickly understand the episode's content and decide if they want to listen to the entire episode. This is especially helpful for new listeners who may not be familiar with the podcast or its hosts.

Show notes also make it easy for listeners to reference specific information or resources mentioned in the episode. For example, if a guest recommends a book or website, the show notes can include a link to that resource. This allows listeners to easily access and engage with the content discussed in the episode.

In addition, show notes can also improve the SEO (search engine optimization) of a podcast's website. By including relevant keywords and phrases in the show notes, the podcast's website can rank higher in search engine results, making it easier for new listeners to find the podcast.

Overall, podcast show notes are an important element of a successful podcast. They help listeners engage with the content, provide a reference for specific information, and can improve the podcast's visibility and reach.

Strategies for creating effective and engaging show notes that provide value to your audience

Creating effective and engaging show notes is an important part of podcasting. Show notes provide your audience with a summary of your episode and additional information that complements the audio content. They also make it easier for listeners to find and revisit the most interesting parts of your podcast. In this chapter, we'll discuss strategies for creating show notes that provide value to your audience.

Start with a Summary
Your show notes should start with a summary of your episode. This summary should provide an overview of the main points you

covered in your podcast. It should be short and to the point, but it should also be descriptive enough to give listeners an idea of what they can expect from the episode. Use a conversational tone, and avoid technical jargon that might confuse your audience.

Include Time Stamps

Adding time stamps to your show notes is an effective way to make it easier for listeners to find the most interesting parts of your podcast. Time stamps indicate where in the episode a particular topic or segment begins and ends. For example, you might include a time stamp like this: "1:02 - Interview with Jane Smith begins." This lets your listeners know exactly where to go to find the information they're looking for.

Add Additional Resources

Your show notes can also include additional resources that complement your episode. This might include links to articles or blog posts that provide more information on a topic you covered in your podcast. You might also include links to other podcasts that cover similar topics. Adding these resources can help your listeners continue to explore the topic and learn more.

Use Visuals

Using visuals in your show notes can make them more engaging and appealing to your audience. This might include images that complement the content of your podcast. For example, if you're talking about a particular book, you might include an image of the book cover. You might also include infographics or other visual aids that help illustrate your points.

Optimize for SEO

Your show notes can also help your podcast get found in search engines. To optimize your show notes for SEO, use descriptive titles and meta descriptions that include keywords related to your topic. Use header tags to break up your content and make it easier to read. And include links to your website or other relevant content.

Overall, creating effective and engaging show notes is an important part of building an engaged audience for your podcast. By providing a summary of your episode, time stamps, additional resources, visuals, and SEO optimization, you can create show notes that provide value to your audience and help your podcast get found in search engines.

I hope you find this chapter helpful in creating effective show notes for your podcast!

Tips for optimizing your show notes for better SEO and searchability

Show notes are an essential component of any podcast episode. They serve as a written summary of the episode's content and help listeners follow along with the discussion. But did you know that show notes can also play a crucial role in search engine optimization (SEO) and the discoverability of your podcast? By optimizing your show notes, you can make it easier for people to find your podcast through search engines and other platforms.

Here are some tips for optimizing your show notes for better SEO and searchability:

Use relevant keywords: Just like with any other type of content, using relevant keywords in your show notes can help them appear in search results. Think about the main topics and themes covered in the episode, and use those keywords throughout the notes. Be sure to use natural language and avoid keyword stuffing, as this can actually hurt your SEO efforts.

Write compelling headlines and descriptions: The headline and description of your episode are the first things people will see when they come across it in search results. Make sure these elements are compelling and accurately represent the content of the episode.

Consider using action-oriented language and incorporating your target keywords.

Link to relevant resources: Including links to relevant resources in your show notes can help boost your SEO and provide additional value to your audience. If you mention a book or website in the episode, be sure to include a link to it in the show notes. This also helps to establish your podcast as a reliable source of information.

Use formatting to your advantage: Using formatting elements like headers, bullet points, and bolded text can make your show notes easier to read and more visually appealing. They can also help search engines better understand the structure and content of your notes, which can improve their searchability.

Include a transcript: Providing a transcript of your episode can be a huge boost to your SEO efforts. Not only does it make your content more accessible to those who are deaf or hard of hearing, but it also gives search engines more text to crawl and index. This can help your podcast show up in search results for more long-tail keywords and phrases.

By following these tips, you can help ensure that your show notes are optimized for SEO and searchability. This can make it easier for people to find your podcast and engage with your content.

Remember, creating engaging and informative show notes can help attract new listeners and keep existing ones coming back for more. So don't overlook this important aspect of your podcasting strategy!

Best Practices for Formatting and Structuring Your Show Notes

Show notes are a critical component of any podcast, providing your listeners with a quick overview of what to expect in your episode and a resource for finding specific information. While the content of your show notes is essential, the way it's formatted and structured is equally important. Well-structured and easy-to-read show notes can make a significant difference in engaging your listeners and driving traffic to your website. In this chapter, we'll discuss some best practices for formatting and structuring your show notes.

Use Headings and Subheadings

Organize your show notes using headings and subheadings to make it easy for your listeners to navigate the content. Headings and subheadings break up your text and make it easier to scan. Use descriptive and keyword-rich headings to provide your listeners with a clear idea of what they can expect from each section.

Keep It Short and Sweet

Show notes are not the place for lengthy descriptions. Instead, focus on providing concise and to-the-point information that summarizes the key points of your podcast episode. Use bullet points to break up long blocks of text and make your show notes easier to read.

Use Images and Multimedia

Including images and multimedia in your show notes can make your content more visually appealing and engaging. Use images, videos, and other multimedia to illustrate your points and help your listeners understand the content better.

Include Timestamps

Timestamps are essential for allowing your listeners to jump to specific parts of your podcast quickly. Use timestamps to indicate where in the episode specific topics or segments begin, making it easier for your listeners to find what they're looking for.

Add Links

Including links in your show notes is an excellent way to provide your listeners with additional resources and information. Include links to your website, social media channels, and any other relevant content.

You can also link to your guests' websites and other relevant sources to provide additional value to your listeners.

Be Consistent
Consistency is essential when it comes to formatting and structuring your show notes. Use a consistent format, style, and tone to create a seamless and cohesive experience for your listeners.

In summary, formatting and structuring your show notes can make a significant difference in engaging your listeners and driving traffic to your website. Use headings and subheadings to organize your content, keep your show notes concise and to the point, use images and multimedia, include timestamps and links, and be consistent in your format, style, and tone. With these best practices, you can create show notes that provide value to your audience and help your podcast stand out.

In conclusion, podcast show notes play a vital role in engaging and growing your audience. They help provide context, value, and searchability to your episodes, as well as enhance your credibility and brand image. By following the strategies and tips outlined in this chapter, you can create effective and engaging show notes that keep your listeners coming back for more. Remember to format your show notes to be easy to read and navigate, optimize them for SEO, and provide value to your audience. With well-crafted show notes, you can maximize the impact of your podcast and build a loyal fanbase.

CHAPTER 21: PROMOTING YOUR PODCAST ON SOCIAL MEDIA

❖ Strategies for creating engaging and shareable content
❖ Tips for using social media to build your audience and connect with your listeners
❖ Best practices for leveraging social media platforms to drive traffic to your podcast and increase downloads
❖ Examples of successful podcasts that have used social media to build a strong following

How to Promote Your Podcast on Social Media
Tips for using social media to build your audience and connect with your listeners
Best practices for leveraging social media platforms to drive traffic to your podcast and increase downloads
Examples of successful podcasts that have used social media to build a strong following

One of the most effective ways to promote your podcast and connect with your audience is through social media. With millions of users on platforms like Facebook, Twitter, and Instagram, social media provides a powerful way to build your brand, increase visibility, and engage with your listeners. In this chapter, we'll explore the strategies, tips, and best practices for using social media to promote your podcast, create engaging content, and build a strong following.
❖

How to Promote Your Podcast on Social Media

Social media can be an incredibly powerful tool for promoting your podcast and reaching a wider audience. Here are some strategies for creating engaging and shareable content that will help you grow your podcast's following on social media.

Create social media accounts for your podcast

The first step to promoting your podcast on social media is to create social media accounts specifically for your podcast. This allows you to share your podcast episodes, engage with your audience, and build a community around your show. Consider creating accounts on popular platforms like Twitter, Facebook, Instagram, and LinkedIn.

Share your episodes on social media

One of the easiest ways to promote your podcast on social media is to share your episodes directly on your social media accounts. You can post links to your latest episodes on Twitter, Facebook, and LinkedIn, or share images and videos on Instagram. Make sure to include eye-catching graphics and catchy captions to grab your audience's attention.

Create engaging social media content

In addition to sharing your podcast episodes, you should also create engaging social media content that will help build your brand and engage with your audience. This could include behind-the-scenes photos and videos, sneak peeks of upcoming episodes, and interesting quotes or statistics related to your show.

Use hashtags and keywords

Hashtags and keywords are an important part of social media marketing, as they help people discover your content. Make sure to include relevant hashtags and keywords in your social media posts to make them more discoverable.

Collaborate with other podcasters and influencers

Collaborating with other podcasters and influencers in your niche can be a great way to promote your podcast to a wider audience. You can collaborate on episodes, guest post on each other's blogs, or simply share each other's content on social media.

Run social media ads

If you have a budget for advertising, running social media ads can be an effective way to promote your podcast to a wider audience. You can target your ads to specific demographics or interests, making them more likely to be seen by people who are interested in your show.

Engage with your audience

Finally, one of the most important things you can do to promote your podcast on social media is to engage with your audience. Respond to comments and messages, ask for feedback, and participate in relevant conversations in your niche. Building a strong community around your podcast can help you grow your following and attract new listeners.

In summary, social media can be an incredibly powerful tool for promoting your podcast and reaching a wider audience. By creating engaging social media content, using hashtags and keywords, collaborating with other podcasters and influencers, running social media ads, and engaging with your audience, you can build a strong following for your podcast on social media.

Tips for using social media to build your audience and connect with your listeners

Social media can be an incredibly powerful tool for promoting your podcast and reaching a wider audience. Here are some strategies for creating engaging and shareable content that will help you grow your podcast's following on social media.

Create social media accounts for your podcast

The first step to promoting your podcast on social media is to create social media accounts specifically for your podcast. This allows you to share your podcast episodes, engage with your audience, and build a community around your show. Consider creating accounts on popular platforms like Twitter, Facebook, Instagram, and LinkedIn.

Share your episodes on social media

One of the easiest ways to promote your podcast on social media is to share your episodes directly on your social media accounts. You can post links to your latest episodes on Twitter, Facebook, and LinkedIn, or share images and videos on Instagram. Make sure to include eye-catching graphics and catchy captions to grab your audience's attention.

Create engaging social media content

In addition to sharing your podcast episodes, you should also create engaging social media content that will help build your brand and engage with your audience. This could include behind-the-scenes photos and videos, sneak peeks of upcoming episodes, and interesting quotes or statistics related to your show.

Use hashtags and keywords

Hashtags and keywords are an important part of social media marketing, as they help people discover your content. Make sure to include relevant hashtags and keywords in your social media posts to make them more discoverable.

Collaborate with other podcasters and influencers

Collaborating with other podcasters and influencers in your niche can be a great way to promote your podcast to a wider audience. You can collaborate on episodes, guest post on each other's blogs, or simply share each other's content on social media.

Run social media ads

If you have a budget for advertising, running social media ads can be an effective way to promote your podcast to a wider audience. You can target your ads to specific demographics or interests, making them more likely to be seen by people who are interested in your show.

Engage with your audience

Finally, one of the most important things you can do to promote your podcast on social media is to engage with your audience. Respond to comments and messages, ask for feedback, and participate in relevant conversations in your niche. Building a strong community around your podcast can help you grow your following and attract new listeners.

In summary, social media can be an incredibly powerful tool for promoting your podcast and reaching a wider audience. By creating engaging social media content, using hashtags and keywords, collaborating with other podcasters and influencers, running social media ads, and engaging with your audience, you can build a strong following for your podcast on social media.

Best practices for leveraging social media platforms to drive traffic to your podcast and increase downloads

Social media can be a powerful tool for promoting your podcast and building your audience. By using social media effectively, you can connect with your listeners, grow your reach, and increase your downloads. Here are some best practices for leveraging social media to drive traffic to your podcast and increase downloads.

Create a social media strategy: Before you start promoting your podcast on social media, it's important to have a plan. Set clear goals, determine your target audience, and decide which platforms you will use. Create a content calendar to help you stay organized and consistent.

Use eye-catching visuals: Social media is a visual medium, so it's important to use eye-catching images and videos that grab your audience's attention. Use high-quality images and graphics that represent your brand and help your posts stand out.

Share teasers and clips: Use social media to tease your upcoming episodes and share clips from past episodes. This can help generate excitement and interest in your podcast, and entice your followers to tune in.

Engage with your audience: Social media is a two-way conversation, so it's important to engage with your audience. Respond to comments and messages, and ask for feedback to create a sense of community and connection with your listeners.

Use hashtags: Hashtags can help your posts get discovered by new audiences, so make sure to use relevant and popular hashtags when promoting your podcast. You can also create your own branded hashtags to help build your brand and create a sense of community.

Collaborate with other creators: Collaborating with other podcasters, bloggers, and influencers can help you reach new audiences and build relationships with other creators. Consider doing guest appearances on other podcasts or hosting joint events to cross-promote your content.

Leverage paid advertising: Social media advertising can be a powerful tool for reaching new audiences and promoting your podcast. Consider using paid advertising on platforms like Facebook and Instagram to target specific audiences and increase your visibility.

By following these best practices, you can leverage social media to drive traffic to your podcast, increase your downloads, and build a strong community of listeners. Remember to stay consistent, engage with your audience, and use social media as a tool to help your podcast grow.

Examples of successful podcasts that have used social media to build a strong following

Social media is an incredibly powerful tool for promoting your podcast and building a strong following. With the right strategy, you can use social media to connect with your audience, increase engagement, and drive more downloads. To help you get started, let's take a look at some examples of successful podcasts that have used social media to build a strong following.

Serial

Serial is one of the most successful podcasts of all time, and a large part of its success can be attributed to its use of social media. The show's producers used Twitter, Facebook, and other social media platforms to create buzz around the show and engage with fans. They also created social media campaigns, such as the #FreeAdnan hashtag, which helped to spread the word about the show and attract new listeners.

My Favorite Murder

My Favorite Murder is a true crime podcast that has become incredibly popular over the past few years. The hosts, Karen Kilgariff and Georgia Hardstark, are known for their engaging personalities and witty banter, and they have used social media to connect with their audience and build a strong following. They regularly post on Instagram, Twitter, and Facebook, sharing behind-the-scenes photos and engaging with fans.

The Joe Rogan Experience

The Joe Rogan Experience is a podcast that covers a wide range of topics, from science and technology to politics and culture. Hosted by comedian and UFC commentator Joe Rogan, the show has built a massive following, in large part due to its presence on social media. Rogan has over 11 million followers on Instagram, where he regularly posts clips from the show and engages with fans.

Radiolab

Radiolab is a science and philosophy podcast that has been around for over a decade. The show's producers have used social media to build a strong following and increase engagement with fans. They regularly post on Twitter and Facebook, sharing behind-the-scenes photos and engaging with listeners. They also created a social media campaign called "Radiolab Bingo," which encouraged fans to share their favorite moments from the show on social media.

Stuff You Should Know

Stuff You Should Know is a podcast that covers a wide range of topics, from science and history to pop culture and current events. The show's hosts, Josh Clark and Chuck Bryant, have used social media to build a strong following and connect with fans. They regularly post on Twitter and Facebook, sharing behind-the-scenes photos and engaging with listeners. They also created a successful social media campaign called "SYSK Selects," which highlighted some of the show's most popular episodes.

These are just a few examples of successful podcasts that have used social media to build a strong following. By following their lead and implementing some of their strategies, you can increase your own podcast's visibility and attract more listeners. Remember to always stay engaged with your audience, be authentic, and create content that resonates with your listeners.

Social media can be a powerful tool for promoting your podcast and building a strong following. By creating engaging content, connecting with your listeners, and leveraging the features and capabilities of different social media platforms, you can increase your visibility, build your brand, and grow your audience. The strategies, tips, and best practices in this chapter will help you get started and make the most of social media for your podcast.

CHAPTER 22: GUEST APPEARANCES AND COLLABORATIONS

❖ How to use guest appearances and collaborations to grow your podcast audience and reach new listeners
❖ Strategies for identifying and reaching out to potential guests and collaborators
❖ Tips for creating engaging and high-quality collaborations that provide value to your audience
❖ Best practices for leveraging guest appearances and collaborations to build your personal brand and grow your podcast

One of the most effective ways to grow your podcast audience and reach new listeners is by leveraging guest appearances and collaborations. By collaborating with other podcasters, thought leaders, and industry experts, you can tap into their existing audiences and gain exposure for your own podcast. But how do you identify potential collaborators and create engaging content that resonates with both of your audiences?

In this chapter, we'll explore strategies for identifying and reaching out to potential guests and collaborators, tips for creating high-quality collaborations that provide value to your audience, and best practices for leveraging guest appearances and collaborations to build your personal brand and grow your podcast.

How to use guest appearances and collaborations to grow your podcast audience and reach new listeners

As a podcaster, one of the best ways to grow your audience and reach new listeners is to collaborate with other podcasters, influencers, and experts in your niche. Guest appearances and collaborations can help you tap into new audiences, build relationships with fellow podcasters, and provide your listeners with fresh perspectives and valuable insights. Here are some strategies for using guest appearances and collaborations to grow your podcast:

Identify potential collaborators: Start by identifying podcasters, influencers, and experts in your niche who have an audience that might be interested in your podcast. Reach out to them via email or social media and introduce yourself, your podcast, and your idea for collaboration. Make sure to personalize your outreach and explain how your collaboration can benefit their audience as well as yours.

Plan your collaboration: Once you've connected with potential collaborators, plan out the details of your collaboration. This could involve co-hosting an episode, conducting an interview, or participating in a roundtable discussion. Make sure to discuss the format, topic, and logistics of your collaboration in advance to ensure that it aligns with your goals and provides value to your audience.

Promote your collaboration: Once your collaboration is live, make sure to promote it on your podcast and social media channels. Encourage your collaborator to do the same, and leverage their audience to reach new listeners. Make sure to provide links and resources that make it easy for listeners to find and subscribe to both podcasts.

Follow up with your collaborator: After your collaboration, make sure to follow up with your collaborator to thank them and discuss the results. Evaluate the success of your collaboration and identify ways to improve for future collaborations.

When done right, guest appearances and collaborations can help you reach new listeners, build your credibility, and grow your audience. By partnering with other podcasters and influencers, you can tap into new audiences and provide valuable content that keeps listeners coming back for more.

Incorporating guest appearances and collaborations into your podcast strategy can help you expand your reach and attract new listeners. By partnering with other podcasters and experts in your niche, you can provide your audience with fresh perspectives and valuable insights, while also tapping into new audiences and building your credibility as a podcaster.

Strategies for identifying and reaching out to potential guests and collaborators

Having guests and collaborators on your podcast can be a powerful way to expand your reach and tap into new audiences. But how do you find the right people to work with and convince them to come on your show? Here are some strategies to consider:

Identify potential guests or collaborators in your niche: Start by brainstorming a list of people who are well-known or respected in your industry or niche. You can also look at other podcasts, blogs, or social media accounts in your space to see who they feature or collaborate with.

Research and reach out to them: Once you have a list of potential guests or collaborators, research them to learn more about their background, expertise, and what they might bring to your show. Use social media or professional networks like LinkedIn to reach out to them with a personalized pitch that explains why you think they would be a good fit for your podcast.

Use your network: Don't underestimate the power of your existing connections. Reach out to people you already know or have worked with in the past and ask if they know anyone who would be a good fit for your show. You can also ask your guests or collaborators to recommend other people they know who would be a good fit.

Attend events: Networking events, conferences, and trade shows are all great places to meet potential guests and collaborators in person. Be sure to bring business cards and be prepared to pitch your podcast and explain why you think working together would be a good opportunity.

Make it easy for them: When you do find someone who is interested in being a guest or collaborator, make the process as easy as possible for them. Provide clear instructions on what you need from them, give them plenty of notice for scheduling, and be flexible with their needs.

By identifying and reaching out to the right guests and collaborators, you can bring fresh perspectives and ideas to your podcast and attract new listeners who are interested in what they have to say.

Tips for creating engaging and high-quality collaborations that provide value to your audience

Collaborating with other podcasters or experts in your field can help you reach a wider audience and provide your listeners with valuable insights and perspectives. However, it's important to approach collaborations with a strategic mindset to ensure that they are successful and beneficial for both parties involved.

Here are some tips for creating engaging and high-quality collaborations that provide value to your audience:

Choose the right collaborators: Before reaching out to potential collaborators, make sure that their expertise and interests align with your podcast's theme and target audience. Look for people who have a similar style and approach to content creation, and who can provide unique perspectives that your listeners will find interesting and valuable.

Plan your collaboration in advance: Take the time to plan out the collaboration in advance, including the topic, format, and timeline. This will help ensure that both parties are on the same page and that the collaboration runs smoothly. Discuss the structure of the episode, the length of the interview, and any specific topics you'd like to cover.

Set clear goals and expectations: Clearly communicate your goals and expectations for the collaboration, including how you plan to promote the episode and how you'd like your collaborator to help promote it as well. Be transparent about your expectations for your collaborator and make sure they have a clear understanding of their role in the collaboration.

Keep the conversation flowing: During the collaboration, focus on having a natural and engaging conversation that keeps the audience interested. Listen actively to your collaborator's responses and ask follow-up questions that delve deeper into the topic. Remember to keep the conversation balanced, allowing your collaborator ample time to share their insights and expertise.

Edit the episode carefully: Once the episode is recorded, take the time to edit it carefully. Cut out any irrelevant or repetitive sections, and ensure that the audio quality is high throughout. Take the time to add relevant show notes and a compelling introduction to draw in new listeners.

Promote the collaboration widely: Promote the collaboration widely across social media channels, email lists, and other online platforms. Encourage your collaborator to do the same, making sure that the episode reaches as many potential listeners as possible.

Overall, collaborations can be a great way to grow your podcast and provide your audience with valuable content. By choosing the right collaborators, planning in advance, and focusing on creating engaging and high-quality content, you can ensure that your collaborations are successful and beneficial for both you and your audience.

Best practices for leveraging guest appearances and collaborations to build your personal brand and grow your podcast

As a podcaster, guest appearances and collaborations can be a powerful way to grow your audience and reach new listeners. By partnering with others in your industry or featuring guests with relevant expertise, you can provide valuable insights and perspectives that your listeners will appreciate.

Here are some best practices for leveraging guest appearances and collaborations to build your personal brand and grow your podcast:

Identify the Right Guests and Collaborators: When seeking out guests and collaborators, look for individuals who have expertise or insights that are relevant to your audience. Consider reaching out to thought leaders in your industry or partnering with other podcasters who have similar audiences. Make sure to also consider the potential benefits to your guests or collaborators, such as exposure to your audience or access to new listeners.

Prepare for Your Collaborations: Before collaborating with others, make sure you have a clear plan for your content and how your collaboration will fit into your overall podcast strategy. Determine the topics and questions you will cover, and consider sharing your notes with your collaborators to ensure everyone is on the same page.

Focus on Value and Engagement: Your goal with guest appearances and collaborations should be to provide value to your listeners and engage them with your content. Make sure your discussions are interesting and informative, and consider sharing takeaways or actionable insights that your listeners can apply to their own lives or businesses.

Promote Your Collaborations: Once your collaboration is published, make sure to promote it through your own channels and social media. Tag your collaborators and encourage them to share the content as well. By cross-promoting your collaborations, you can reach a wider audience and increase the visibility of your podcast.

Follow Up with Your Collaborators: After your collaboration is published, make sure to follow up with your collaborators and thank them for their time and insights. Consider building relationships with your collaborators over time, as they may be interested in collaborating with you again in the future.

By following these best practices for leveraging guest appearances and collaborations, you can build your personal brand, grow your podcast audience, and provide value to your listeners. Keep in mind that collaborations and guest appearances are just one part of your overall podcast strategy, so make sure to integrate them in a way that aligns with your goals and objectives.

Incorporating guest appearances and collaborations into your podcasting strategy can help you grow your audience and expand your reach in a meaningful way. By creating engaging content that provides value to your listeners, you can establish yourself as a thought leader in your industry and build your personal brand. As you continue to collaborate with other podcasters and industry experts, you'll gain valuable insights and experiences that can help you improve your own podcast and create even more compelling content for your audience. So don't be afraid to reach out and start collaborating – you never know what opportunities it might lead to!

CHAPTER 23: BUILDING A STRONG PODCAST COMMUNITY

❖ Importance of building a strong and engaged podcast community
❖ Strategies for engaging with your audience and building relationships with your listeners
❖ Tips for creating a sense of community and belonging among your listeners
❖ Best practices for using your podcast to drive positive change and make a difference in your listeners' lives

As a podcaster, building a strong and engaged community around your show is one of the most rewarding experiences you can have. Not only does it allow you to connect with your listeners on a deeper level, but it also provides an opportunity to create positive change in their lives. In this chapter, we will explore the importance of building a podcast community and discuss strategies for engaging with your audience, creating a sense of belonging, and making a positive impact.

Importance of building a strong and engaged podcast community

Podcasting is more than just creating and publishing audio content. One of the most important aspects of a successful podcast is building a strong and engaged community of listeners who are invested in your show and its message. A podcast community can provide valuable feedback, help promote your show, and even become a source of revenue through merchandise sales, sponsorships, and crowdfunding.

So, why is building a strong and engaged podcast community so important? Here are a few key reasons:

Provides valuable feedback: A strong podcast community can provide valuable feedback on your show. They can tell you what they like, what they don't like, and what they want to hear more of. This feedback can help you improve your show and make it more appealing to your audience.

Helps promote your show: Your podcast community can help spread the word about your show through social media, word of mouth, and other channels. They can also leave reviews and ratings on podcast directories, which can help increase your visibility and reach new listeners.

Creates a sense of belonging: Building a strong podcast community can help create a sense of belonging for your listeners. They can feel like they are part of a larger community that shares their interests and values. This can help foster loyalty and encourage listeners to continue tuning in to your show.

Can lead to revenue opportunities: A strong and engaged podcast community can lead to revenue opportunities, such as sponsorships, merchandise sales, and crowdfunding campaigns. This can help support your show and allow you to continue creating content that resonates with your audience.

Now that you understand the importance of building a strong and engaged podcast community, let's explore some strategies for doing just that.

Stay tuned for the next sections where we will discuss how to build a podcast community, engage with your listeners, and maintain their loyalty.

Strategies for engaging with your audience and building relationships with your listeners

Engaging with your audience is a crucial aspect of building a successful podcast. Not only does it create a sense of community and connection, but it can also lead to increased downloads, positive reviews, and word-of-mouth marketing. Here are some strategies for engaging with your audience and building relationships with your listeners:

Encourage feedback: Ask your audience to leave reviews, send emails, or connect with you on social media to provide feedback on your podcast. Make it clear that you value their input and want to hear their thoughts.

Respond to feedback: When you receive feedback from your audience, make sure to respond in a timely and thoughtful manner. Whether it's a positive comment or constructive criticism, responding shows that you care about your listeners and are invested in their experience.

Create a community: Consider creating a private Facebook group, Discord server, or other online space where your listeners can connect with each other and with you. This can foster a sense of community and allow you to build deeper relationships with your audience.

Feature listener questions and comments: Incorporate listener questions, comments, and feedback into your podcast episodes. This shows that you're paying attention to your audience and value their contributions.

Offer exclusive content: Consider offering exclusive content, such as bonus episodes, Q&A sessions, or early access to new episodes, to your most dedicated listeners. This can help to build loyalty and keep your audience engaged.

Collaborate with listeners: Invite listeners to be guests on your podcast or participate in Q&A sessions. This can create a sense of investment and ownership among your audience and foster a deeper connection with your listeners.

Attend events: Consider attending events related to your podcast's niche or topic. This can give you the opportunity to meet your listeners in person, network with other podcasters, and promote your podcast to a wider audience.

By using these strategies, you can create a strong and engaged podcast community that will help to grow your podcast and create a loyal following.

Tips for creating a sense of community and belonging among your listeners

Creating a community of listeners is an essential aspect of building a successful podcast. A strong and engaged community can provide valuable feedback, support, and even help to spread the word about your podcast to a wider audience. Here are some tips for creating a sense of community and belonging among your listeners.

Encourage listener feedback and participation: Make it easy for your listeners to provide feedback and participate in discussions. This can be done through social media, email, or even a dedicated discussion forum or Discord server. Respond promptly to listener feedback and let them know that you value their opinions.

Create a brand personality: Your podcast should have a distinct personality that reflects your brand and values. This can include a consistent tone, visual style, and even catchphrases or running jokes. By creating a strong brand personality, you can build a sense of familiarity and belonging among your listeners.

Offer exclusive content or perks: Offer exclusive content or perks to your most engaged listeners. This can include bonus episodes, early access to episodes, or even merchandise. By providing added value to your most dedicated listeners, you can help to create a sense of exclusivity and belonging.

Host live events: Hosting live events, such as Q&A sessions or meet-and-greets, can be a great way to connect with your listeners in person. This can help to foster a sense of community and give your listeners a chance to meet other fans of your podcast.

Collaborate with other podcasts: Collaborating with other podcasts in your niche can be a great way to cross-promote your show and introduce your audience to new voices and perspectives. By working together, you can build a stronger podcast community and help to grow the overall audience for your niche.

By implementing these tips, you can create a sense of community and belonging among your listeners, which can help to drive engagement and grow your audience over time.

Overall, building a strong and engaged podcast community requires time and effort, but the benefits can be immense. By fostering a sense of belonging and offering added value to your most dedicated listeners, you can create a loyal and supportive community that can help to take your podcast to the next level.

Best practices for using your podcast to drive positive change and make a difference in your listeners' lives

Podcasts have become a powerful medium for influencing positive change and making a difference in people's lives. Whether it's through education, inspiration, or motivation, podcasts have the potential to impact listeners on a deep and personal level. In this chapter, we'll explore some best practices for using your podcast to drive positive change and make a difference in your listeners' lives.

Identify your purpose: Before you start your podcast, you need to identify your purpose. What do you want to achieve with your podcast? What positive change do you want to make in your listeners' lives? Once you have a clear purpose in mind, you can develop your content and strategy accordingly.

Provide value: Your podcast should provide real value to your listeners. Whether it's through educational content, inspirational stories, or practical advice, your podcast should aim to help your listeners in some way. When you provide value, you build trust and credibility with your audience.

Be authentic: Authenticity is key to building a strong connection with your audience. Be genuine and sincere in your approach, and let your personality shine through. Share your own experiences and struggles, and be open about your own journey.

Focus on your niche: To make a real impact, it's important to focus on your niche. Identify a specific topic or area of interest and create content that speaks directly to that audience. When you focus on a specific niche, you'll build a loyal following of listeners who share your passion.

Create a sense of community: Building a sense of community is a great way to engage your listeners and make a real difference in their lives. Encourage your listeners to share their own stories and experiences, and create opportunities for them to connect with each other. This could be through social media, live events, or other forms of interaction.

Collaborate with other influencers: Collaborating with other influencers is a great way to reach new audiences and make a greater impact. Find other podcasters, bloggers, or social media influencers who share your values and message, and explore opportunities for collaboration.

Take action: To drive real change, it's important to take action. Use your platform to raise awareness of important issues, promote positive initiatives, and encourage your listeners to get involved. By taking action, you'll inspire your listeners to do the same and create a ripple effect of positive change.

In summary, using your podcast to drive positive change and make a difference in your listeners' lives requires a clear purpose, authentic approach, and a focus on providing real value. By creating a sense of community, collaborating with other influencers, and taking action, you can make a real impact and inspire positive change in the world.

Building a strong and engaged podcast community is a long-term process that requires dedication, effort, and a genuine passion for your show and your audience. By using the strategies, tips, and best practices discussed in this chapter, you can cultivate a loyal following that will support your show, spread the word about it, and make a real difference in the world. Remember, the key to building a successful podcast community is to focus on creating valuable content, engaging with your audience, and always being open to feedback and suggestions.

CHAPTER 24: MONETIZATION STRATEGIES

❖ Overview of Different Monetization Strategies for Podcasts

❖ Strategies for choosing the right monetization strategy for your podcast and audience

❖ Tips for implementing and optimizing your monetization strategy to generate revenue from your podcast

❖ Best practices for managing your podcast business finances and scaling your podcast for future growth

Overview of Different Monetization Strategies for Podcasts

Podcasting can be a great hobby or a way to build a brand, but it can also be a lucrative business opportunity. There are many ways to monetize your podcast and turn it into a profitable venture. In this chapter, we will discuss some popular monetization strategies for podcasts.

Sponsorship and Advertising

One of the most common ways to monetize a podcast is through sponsorships and advertising. This involves partnering with brands and businesses that want to reach your audience. You can either read a pre-written ad during your podcast or create your own ad to promote the sponsor's product or service. You can charge a fee per episode or per campaign, depending on the size of your audience.

Patreon

Patreon is a popular crowdfunding platform that allows fans to support their favorite creators with monthly contributions. As a podcaster, you can offer exclusive content, early access to episodes, merchandise, and other perks to your patrons. This can provide a stable source of income and help you fund your podcast's production costs.

Merchandise Sales

If you have a dedicated audience, you can sell branded merchandise such as T-shirts, hats, and mugs. This can help you generate additional revenue and provide your listeners with a way to show their support.

Personal Branding

As a podcaster, you can use your platform to build your personal brand and offer services such as coaching, consulting, or public speaking. This can help you leverage your expertise and experience to generate income outside of your podcast.

While these are some of the most popular monetization strategies for podcasts, it's important to keep in mind that each strategy has its own advantages and disadvantages. It's important to choose the right strategy for your podcast based on your goals, audience, and brand.

In the next chapter, we will dive deeper into some of these strategies and provide tips on how to successfully monetize your podcast.

Strategies for choosing the right monetization strategy for your podcast and audience

When it comes to choosing a monetization strategy for your podcast, there are several options to consider. Some of the most common monetization strategies include sponsorship and advertising, Patreon, merchandise sales, and personal branding. Here are some strategies to help you choose the right one for your podcast and audience:

Understand your audience: Before you choose a monetization strategy, you need to have a deep understanding of your audience. What are their interests, preferences, and behaviors? What kind of content resonates with them? Understanding your audience will help you choose a monetization strategy that is a good fit for their needs and interests.

Evaluate your content: You should also evaluate your content to determine what monetization strategies will work best for your podcast. For example, if you have a highly engaged audience that is interested in supporting your work, Patreon or merchandise sales may be a good fit. On the other hand, if you have a large audience with a broad demographic, sponsorship and advertising may be a better choice.

Consider your niche: Your podcast's niche can also influence your monetization strategy. If your podcast is focused on a specific topic or industry, you may have more success with sponsorships and advertising from companies in that industry. If you have a loyal audience that is interested in the topic, merchandise sales or Patreon may also be a good fit.

Test different strategies: It's important to test different monetization strategies to see what works best for your audience and podcast. Don't be afraid to experiment with different approaches to find the right fit.

Focus on building your audience: No matter what monetization strategy you choose, building your audience should be your top priority. The larger and more engaged your audience is, the more opportunities you'll have to monetize your podcast.

By considering your audience, content, niche, testing different strategies, and focusing on building your audience, you can choose the right monetization strategy for your podcast and grow your revenue over time.

Tips for implementing and optimizing your monetization strategy to generate revenue from your podcast

Once you've chosen a monetization strategy for your podcast, it's time to put it into action. Here are some tips for implementing and optimizing your monetization strategy to generate revenue from your podcast:

Develop a plan: Before you start implementing your monetization strategy, develop a plan that outlines your goals, target audience, and the steps you'll take to achieve those goals. Your plan should also include a timeline for each step, so you can track your progress and adjust your strategy as needed.

Use multiple monetization strategies: Don't rely on just one monetization strategy. Instead, use multiple strategies to diversify your revenue streams and increase your chances of success. For example, you can use sponsorship and advertising, Patreon, merchandise sales, and personal branding together to generate more revenue.

Understand your audience: To effectively monetize your podcast, you need to understand your audience and what they're interested in. Conduct surveys or polls, engage with your listeners on social media, and track your download and engagement data to get a better understanding of your audience.

Choose the right sponsorships and advertisers: When selecting sponsorships and advertisers, make sure they align with your podcast's values and content. You don't want to promote products or services that your audience won't find relevant or helpful.

Create engaging ads: Whether you're doing pre-roll or mid-roll ads, make sure they're engaging and provide value to your listeners. Avoid generic or canned ads, and personalize them to fit your audience.

Be transparent: Transparency is key when it comes to monetization. Let your audience know when you're promoting sponsored products or services, and be clear about your monetization strategy. If you're using Patreon or other donation-based models, be transparent about how the money will be used.

Offer exclusive content: If you're using Patreon or other donation-based models, offer exclusive content to your subscribers. This can be additional episodes, early access to content, or behind-the-scenes content that's not available to the general public.

Create high-quality merchandise: If you're selling merchandise, make sure it's high-quality and something your audience will want to buy. Use your podcast's branding and logo to create unique and eye-catching merchandise.

Build a personal brand: If you're using personal branding as a monetization strategy, make sure to build a strong and consistent personal brand. Use social media to promote yourself and your podcast, and engage with your audience to build a loyal following.

Continuously track and optimize your strategy: Finally, it's important to continuously track and optimize your monetization strategy. Keep an eye on your revenue streams, track your audience engagement, and adjust your strategy as needed to maximize your revenue.

By implementing these tips, you can effectively monetize your podcast and generate revenue from your hard work and dedication.

In conclusion, there are many different monetization strategies you can use to generate revenue from your podcast, and it's important to choose the right strategy for your audience and goals. Whether you're using sponsorship and advertising, Patreon, merchandise sales, personal branding, or a combination of these strategies, it's crucial to understand your audience, be transparent, and continuously track and optimize your strategy to maximize your revenue. By implementing these tips, you can effectively monetize your podcast and turn it into a sustainable and profitable venture.

Best practices for managing your podcast business finances and scaling your podcast for future growth

As your podcast grows and begins to generate revenue, it's essential to manage your finances properly to ensure the long-term success of your podcast. Here are some best practices for managing your podcast business finances and scaling your podcast for future growth.

Track your income and expenses
To effectively manage your podcast finances, you need to track all of your income and expenses. This includes revenue from sponsorships and merchandise sales, as well as any expenses such as hosting fees, equipment costs, and advertising. Use a spreadsheet or accounting software to track your income and expenses and ensure that you stay on top of your finances.

Create a budget
Creating a budget is an essential step in managing your podcast finances. Start by looking at your historical income and expenses and use that data to create a budget for the upcoming months or year. Be sure to include all of your expected income and expenses, including any planned investments or upgrades.

Plan for taxes
As a business owner, you'll need to pay taxes on your podcast income. Make sure you understand the tax laws in your country and set aside money each month to cover your tax liabilities. It's a good idea to work with a tax professional to ensure that you're handling your taxes correctly.

Diversify your revenue streams
To ensure the long-term success of your podcast, it's essential to diversify your revenue streams. Don't rely solely on sponsorships or

advertising. Consider offering additional products or services that align with your podcast, such as merchandise, consulting services, or courses.

Invest in your podcast

To continue growing your podcast, you'll need to invest in it. This might mean upgrading your equipment, hiring a team to help with editing and production, or investing in marketing or advertising. Be sure to budget for these expenses and make strategic investments that will help you achieve your growth goals.

Scale your podcast strategically

Scaling your podcast means growing your audience and increasing your revenue over time. It's essential to scale your podcast strategically to ensure that you don't overextend yourself financially or compromise the quality of your podcast. As you grow your podcast, continue to evaluate your revenue and expenses and make adjustments as needed.

Conclusion

Managing your podcast business finances is critical to the long-term success of your podcast. By tracking your income and expenses, creating a budget, planning for taxes, diversifying your revenue streams, investing in your podcast, and scaling strategically, you can set yourself up for success and continue to grow your podcast for years to come.

CHAPTER 25: SPONSORSHIP AND ADVERTISING

❖ What are sponsorships and how do they work?
❖ Strategies for identifying and approaching potential sponsors for your podcast
❖ Tips for creating effective sponsorship pitches and negotiating deals with sponsors
❖ Best practices for incorporating sponsored content into your podcast in a way that resonates with your audience

Sponsorships can be a significant source of revenue for podcasters, but they require careful consideration and execution to be effective. In this chapter, we will discuss what sponsorships are and how they work. We will also explore strategies for identifying and approaching potential sponsors, as well as tips for creating effective sponsorship pitches and negotiating deals. Finally, we will examine best practices for incorporating sponsored content into your podcast in a way that resonates with your audience.

What are sponsorships and how do they work?

In the world of podcasting, sponsorships are a common way to generate revenue. Essentially, a sponsorship is when a company pays you to promote their product or service on your podcast. This can take the form of a brief ad spot or mention during your podcast episode.

Sponsorships work by establishing a partnership between you and the sponsoring company. They will provide you with a script or guidelines for what they would like you to say during the ad spot. In some cases, they may even provide you with a pre-recorded audio clip to include in your podcast.

Once you have recorded the ad spot, you will typically send it to the sponsoring company for approval. Once they have given their approval, you can include the ad spot in your podcast episode and collect payment for your sponsorship.

Sponsorship rates can vary widely depending on factors such as your podcast's size and niche, the sponsoring company's budget, and the length and frequency of the ad spot. Some sponsorships may be a one-time deal, while others may be ongoing partnerships.

Overall, sponsorships can be a great way to generate revenue for your podcast while also providing value to your listeners by introducing them to products or services they may be interested in.

Strategies for identifying and approaching potential sponsors for your podcast

One of the most popular ways to monetize your podcast is through sponsorships, where companies pay you to promote their products or services during your show. To secure sponsorships, you need to identify potential sponsors and pitch your podcast to them. Here are some strategies for identifying and approaching potential sponsors for your podcast:

Identify potential sponsors: Start by researching companies that are relevant to your podcast's niche and target audience. Look for companies that have products or services that align with your podcast's theme and values. You can use tools like Google, LinkedIn, and social media platforms to identify potential sponsors.

Build relationships: Once you have identified potential sponsors, start building relationships with them. Follow them on social media, subscribe to their email newsletters, and engage with their content. This will help you understand their brand and values and make it easier to pitch your podcast to them.

Create a sponsorship package: Develop a sponsorship package that outlines the benefits of sponsoring your podcast. The package should include information about your podcast's audience, the reach of your podcast, the demographics of your audience, and the benefits that the sponsor will receive from sponsoring your podcast.

Reach out to sponsors: Once you have created your sponsorship package, reach out to potential sponsors via email or social media. Start by introducing yourself and your podcast, and explain why you think your podcast would be a good fit for their brand. Be sure to include your sponsorship package in your pitch.

Negotiate the terms: If a sponsor is interested in working with you, you will need to negotiate the terms of the sponsorship agreement. This includes the length of the sponsorship, the number of ads you will run, the price of the sponsorship, and any other terms that are relevant to the agreement.

Deliver on your promises: Once you have secured a sponsorship, it's important to deliver on your promises. Make sure that you run the agreed-upon number of ads during your podcast, and promote the sponsor on your social media channels and website.

By following these strategies, you can identify and approach potential sponsors for your podcast and secure valuable sponsorships that can help you monetize your show and grow your audience.

Tips for creating effective sponsorship pitches and negotiating deals with sponsors

Podcast sponsorships are a great way to monetize your podcast and bring in revenue. But in order to secure sponsorships, you need to create effective pitches that will capture the attention of potential sponsors and convince them that your podcast is the right fit for their brand. Here are some tips for creating effective sponsorship pitches and negotiating deals with sponsors:

Know your audience: Before you start pitching to potential sponsors, it's important to have a clear understanding of your audience. This includes their demographics, interests, and buying habits. By understanding your audience, you can better position your podcast to potential sponsors and demonstrate the value that your podcast can offer to their brand.

Identify potential sponsors: Research potential sponsors that align with your podcast's content and audience. Look for companies that are already advertising in your industry and reach out to them with a customized pitch.

Create a sponsorship package: Develop a sponsorship package that outlines the different sponsorship levels, the benefits that sponsors will receive, and the pricing for each level. Make sure to include a clear call-to-action that prompts potential sponsors to get in touch with you to learn more.

Tailor your pitch: Customize your pitch for each potential sponsor. Highlight how your podcast aligns with their brand, and what unique value your podcast can offer to their audience.

Be clear about the benefits: Make sure to clearly articulate the benefits of sponsoring your podcast. This could include mentions in your podcast episodes, advertising space on your website or social media platforms, or other promotional opportunities.

Negotiate the terms: Once a potential sponsor is interested, it's time to negotiate the terms of the sponsorship. Make sure to clearly outline the deliverables and expectations for both parties, and set a clear timeline for when the sponsorship will begin and end.

Follow up and deliver: Once the deal is finalized, make sure to follow up with the sponsor and deliver on your commitments. This includes including sponsor mentions in your podcast episodes, promoting their brand on your social media channels, and any other agreed-upon deliverables.

By following these tips, you can create effective sponsorship pitches and secure sponsorship deals that will help you monetize your podcast and bring in revenue.

Best practices for incorporating sponsored content into your podcast in a way that resonates with your audience

When it comes to incorporating sponsored content into your podcast, it's important to strike a balance between providing value to your sponsor and maintaining your authenticity and credibility with your audience. Here are some best practices for incorporating sponsored content into your podcast:

Choose sponsors that align with your brand and values: When considering potential sponsors, make sure they align with the values and topics of your podcast. You want to make sure that any products or services you promote are something your audience is likely to be interested in, and that you can genuinely recommend.

Integrate sponsored content in a natural and authentic way: The best sponsored content doesn't sound like an ad, but rather a seamless part of the conversation. Try to integrate the sponsored content in a way that sounds natural, such as sharing a personal experience using the product or service.

Be transparent with your audience: It's important to be transparent with your audience about sponsored content. Disclose any sponsored content upfront, so your audience knows what to expect. This builds trust and helps your audience understand that you are being upfront about your relationship with the sponsor.

Create a unique value proposition for your sponsor: When pitching to sponsors, it's important to create a unique value proposition that shows how your podcast and audience can provide value to the sponsor. This can include things like the size and demographics of your audience, engagement metrics, and the creative ways in which you plan to incorporate the sponsored content.

Set clear expectations with sponsors: When negotiating with sponsors, make sure to set clear expectations around the content and the length of the sponsorship. This can help avoid any misunderstandings or miscommunication down the line.

Measure the success of sponsored content: Once the sponsored content has been published, make sure to measure its success. This can include tracking metrics such as click-through rates, conversions, and engagement. Use this information to refine and improve future sponsored content.

By following these best practices, you can create sponsored content that resonates with your audience and provides value to your sponsor. Remember, authenticity and transparency are key to maintaining your credibility with your audience while also generating revenue for your podcast.

Sponsorships can provide a valuable source of revenue for podcasters, but it's important to approach them with careful consideration and a thoughtful strategy. By identifying potential sponsors, crafting effective pitches, and incorporating sponsored content in a way that resonates with your audience, you can create a win-win situation for both you and your sponsors. By following the best practices outlined in this chapter, you can successfully monetize your podcast while still providing high-quality content that your listeners enjoy.

CHAPTER 26: CREATING A PATREON CAMPAIGN

❖ What is Patreon and how does it work?
❖ Strategies for creating and launching a successful Patreon campaign for your podcast
❖ Tips for engaging and rewarding your Patreon supporters to build a strong and loyal fanbase
❖ Best practices for managing your Patreon campaign and scaling it for future growth

As a podcaster, you may be looking for ways to monetize your content and generate revenue to support your show. One popular platform for doing so is Patreon, which allows fans to support creators with regular payments in exchange for exclusive content and perks. In this chapter, we'll explore what Patreon is and how it works, as well as strategies for creating and launching a successful campaign for your podcast. We'll also offer tips for engaging and rewarding your Patreon supporters, and best practices for managing and growing your Patreon presence over time.

What is Patreon and how does it work?

Patreon is a membership platform that allows creators, including podcasters, to earn recurring income from their work. It provides a way for your listeners to support your podcast financially while also providing them with exclusive content and perks.

So, how does Patreon work? First, you create a page on the platform and describe your podcast and the benefits that patrons will receive when they support you. You can offer a variety of rewards, such as early access to new episodes, bonus episodes, exclusive merchandise, and behind-the-scenes content.

Next, you set up different membership tiers, each with its own rewards and price point. For example, you might have a $5/month tier that gives access to bonus content and a $15/month tier that includes a monthly Q&A session with you.

Your listeners can then choose to become patrons by subscribing to one of your membership tiers. They can cancel or change their subscription at any time, and you can communicate with your patrons and manage your rewards through the Patreon platform.

Patreon takes a 5% commission on all pledges, and there may be additional payment processing fees depending on the payment method. However, the platform provides a simple and streamlined way to earn recurring income from your podcast and build a community of supporters.

If you're considering using Patreon for your podcast, here are some strategies to keep in mind:

Clearly communicate the benefits of becoming a patron. Make sure your potential supporters understand what they'll get in return for their financial contribution, and emphasize the exclusive and personalized nature of the rewards.

Create rewards that are scalable and sustainable. Make sure that the rewards you offer are manageable for you and your team, and that they can be scaled as your number of patrons grows.

Offer regular and consistent rewards. Make sure that your patrons receive their rewards on a regular and predictable schedule, and communicate any changes to your reward system clearly.

Foster a sense of community among your patrons. Use Patreon as an opportunity to build a community around your podcast, by encouraging interaction and feedback between you and your patrons.

By using Patreon, you can create a more sustainable and reliable income stream for your podcast, while also offering your listeners a more personal and exclusive connection to your content.

Strategies for creating and launching a successful Patreon campaign for your podcast

Strategies for Creating and Launching a Successful Patreon Campaign for Your Podcast

Patreon is a popular platform that enables creators to get paid by fans for the content they create. Many podcasters use Patreon to generate revenue from their podcast and build a community around their show. Here are some strategies for creating and launching a successful Patreon campaign for your podcast:

1. Determine Your Goals and Objectives

Before you start creating your Patreon campaign, it's important to determine your goals and objectives. Ask yourself why you want to use Patreon to monetize your podcast. Is it to generate additional revenue? Or to build a community around your show? Having a clear understanding of your goals and objectives will help you create a campaign that resonates with your audience.

2. Choose the Right Tier System

Patreon allows creators to offer different tiers of membership to their fans. When creating your Patreon campaign, it's important to choose the right tier system that aligns with your goals and objectives. You can offer different levels of membership that come with different benefits, such as bonus episodes, merchandise, or exclusive access to behind-the-scenes content.

3. Create Compelling Content and Rewards

One of the most important factors in the success of your Patreon campaign is the content and rewards you offer to your fans. You should aim to create content and rewards that are exclusive and compelling.

This can include bonus episodes, Q&A sessions, merchandise, and exclusive access to your community.

4. Promote Your Patreon Campaign

Promoting your Patreon campaign is essential to its success. You should use your social media channels, email list, and podcast episodes to promote your campaign and encourage your fans to support your show. You can also collaborate with other podcasters or influencers in your niche to promote your Patreon campaign.

5. Engage with Your Patrons

Engaging with your patrons is crucial to building a strong community around your podcast. You should regularly communicate with your patrons and keep them updated on the latest developments with your show. You can also use Patreon's messaging system to send personalized messages to your patrons and provide them with additional value.

6. Continuously Evaluate and Optimize Your Campaign

It's important to continuously evaluate and optimize your Patreon campaign to ensure its success. You should regularly review your campaign's performance and make changes as necessary to improve its effectiveness. This can include adjusting your tier system, updating your content and rewards, and improving your promotional strategies.

By following these strategies, you can create and launch a successful Patreon campaign for your podcast that generates revenue and builds a strong community around your show.

Conclusion

Patreon is a powerful tool for monetizing your podcast and building a community around your show. By determining your goals and objectives, choosing the right tier system, creating compelling content and rewards, promoting your campaign, engaging with your patrons, and continuously evaluating and optimizing your campaign, you can create a successful Patreon campaign that generates revenue and provides value to your audience.

Tips for engaging and rewarding your Patreon supporters to build a strong and loyal fanbase

One of the keys to building a successful Patreon campaign for your podcast is to offer engaging and rewarding content to your supporters. By providing value and incentives to your Patreon community, you can foster a strong and loyal fanbase that will support your podcast for the long-term. Here are some tips for engaging and rewarding your Patreon supporters:

Offer exclusive content: One of the most effective ways to engage your Patreon supporters is to offer them exclusive content that they can't find anywhere else. This can include early access to new episodes, behind-the-scenes content, Q&A sessions, and more. By providing exclusive content, you can make your supporters feel like they're part of a special community that gets access to unique and valuable content.

Provide perks and rewards: In addition to exclusive content, you can also offer perks and rewards to your Patreon supporters. This can include things like merchandise, shoutouts on your podcast, personalized messages, and more. The key is to offer rewards that are meaningful and relevant to your supporters, so they feel appreciated and valued for their contributions.

Engage with your supporters: Building a strong and engaged community on Patreon requires more than just offering exclusive content and perks. You also need to actively engage with your supporters and make them feel like they're part of the conversation. This can include responding to comments and messages, hosting live Q&A sessions, and soliciting feedback from your supporters on what they'd like to see from your Patreon campaign.

Recognize and thank your supporters: It's important to regularly recognize and thank your Patreon supporters for their contributions. This can include shoutouts on your podcast, personalized messages, and public acknowledgments on your social media channels. By recognizing your supporters, you can make them feel appreciated and valued, which will encourage them to continue supporting your podcast.

Continuously improve your offerings: To keep your Patreon supporters engaged and interested, it's important to continuously improve your offerings and provide new and exciting content. This can include experimenting with new formats, introducing new perks and rewards, and seeking feedback from your supporters on what they'd like to see more of. By constantly striving to improve your Patreon campaign, you can keep your supporters engaged and invested in your podcast.

By following these tips, you can build a strong and loyal Patreon community that will support your podcast for the long-term. Remember to always provide value and incentives to your supporters, engage with them regularly, and continuously improve your offerings to keep them interested and invested in your podcast.

Best practices for managing your Patreon campaign and scaling it for future growth

Once you've launched your Patreon campaign, it's important to manage it effectively in order to retain your supporters and continue to grow your fanbase. Here are some best practices to keep in mind:

Keep your content consistent: One of the biggest reasons people will support you on Patreon is because they love your content. Make sure you are delivering on your promises and providing regular content updates. You can use the Patreon platform to schedule your content, which can help you stay on track and keep your patrons happy.

Provide unique perks: One of the best ways to encourage people to become a patron is to offer unique perks that they can't get anywhere else. Consider offering early access to episodes, exclusive content, or even one-on-one video calls with your supporters. This will help your patrons feel like they are part of an exclusive community and will keep them coming back for more.

Engage with your supporters: Make sure you are interacting with your supporters on a regular basis. Respond to comments and messages, ask for feedback, and provide updates on your progress. This will help your patrons feel like they are part of the process and will encourage them to continue to support you.

Monitor your analytics: Patreon provides detailed analytics that can help you understand your audience and their behavior. Make sure you are regularly monitoring your analytics to see what content is resonating with your supporters, what perks are most popular, and where your patrons are coming from.

Be transparent: Transparency is key when it comes to managing a Patreon campaign. Make sure you are clear about what your supporters can expect from you and where their money is going. Provide regular updates on how the campaign is progressing and how the funds are being used. This will help build trust with your supporters and encourage them to continue to support you.

Scale your campaign: Once you've built a strong Patreon community, consider expanding your campaign to reach a wider audience. You can do this by offering new perks or creating different tiers of support. Just make sure you are providing value to your supporters and that you are not spreading yourself too thin.

By following these best practices, you can effectively manage your Patreon campaign and continue to grow your podcast audience. Remember, the key to success is to provide value to your supporters and to stay engaged with your community.

If you're looking for a way to monetize your podcast and build a closer relationship with your fans, Patreon can be a powerful tool. By creating exclusive content and perks for your supporters, you can generate a reliable source of income while also building a strong and loyal fanbase. To make the most of Patreon, be sure to carefully plan and launch your campaign, engage with your supporters regularly, and continually look for ways to provide more value to your community. With the right approach, you can use Patreon to grow your podcast and support your creative endeavors for years to come.

CHAPTER 27: SELLING MERCHANDISE

❖ How to create and sell merchandise related to your podcast, including t-shirts, mugs, and other items
❖ Strategies for identifying and selecting the right merchandise to sell to your audience
❖ Tips for promoting your merchandise and encouraging your listeners to make purchases
❖ Best practices for managing your merchandise sales and fulfillment process

In today's digital age, creating and selling merchandise related to your podcast can be a great way to generate revenue and grow your brand. With so many options available, from t-shirts and mugs to phone cases and stickers, the possibilities are endless. In this chapter, we will explore strategies for identifying and selecting the right merchandise, as well as tips for promoting your products and managing your sales and fulfillment process.

How to create and sell merchandise related to your podcast, including t-shirts, mugs, and other items

Creating and selling merchandise related to your podcast can be a great way to not only generate additional income but also increase brand recognition and engagement with your audience. In this chapter, we'll discuss the steps you can take to create and sell merchandise related to your podcast.

Step 1: Identify Your Brand

Before creating merchandise, you need to identify your brand. Your brand is what makes your podcast unique and recognizable. It's important to have a clear idea of what your brand is and how you want to communicate it through merchandise.

Step 2: Decide on Merchandise Ideas

Once you've identified your brand, brainstorm merchandise ideas that align with it. Consider items such as t-shirts, hoodies, hats, mugs, stickers, and phone cases. You can also think outside the box and create unique items that relate to your podcast's subject matter.

Step 3: Find a Merchandise Provider

There are several merchandise providers that can help you create and sell your products. Consider using a print-on-demand service such as Printful, TeeSpring, or Redbubble. These services allow you to create designs and upload them to their platform, and they handle the printing, shipping, and payment processing.

Step 4: Design Your Merchandise

Use your brand identity to design merchandise that resonates with your audience. Ensure that the designs are unique, high-quality, and visually appealing. You can hire a freelance designer or create the designs yourself using graphic design software such as Canva or Adobe Illustrator.

Step 5: Set Prices and Launch Your Merchandise

Set a fair price for your merchandise that reflects the cost of production, shipping, and any additional fees. Once you've decided on pricing, you can launch your merchandise and promote it to your audience through your podcast, website, and social media channels.

Step 6: Engage With Your Customers

Engage with your customers by providing excellent customer service, responding to their inquiries promptly, and thanking them for their support. You can also encourage them to share photos of themselves using or wearing your merchandise on social media, which can help to promote your podcast.

In conclusion, creating and selling merchandise related to your podcast can be a fun and profitable way to engage with your audience and promote your brand. By following these steps, you can create high-quality merchandise that resonates with your audience and generates additional revenue for your podcast.

Strategies for identifying and selecting the right merchandise to sell to your audience

Creating and selling merchandise related to your podcast can be a great way to generate revenue and connect with your audience. However, with so many products and options available, it can be challenging to decide on the right merchandise to offer.

Here are some strategies for identifying and selecting the right merchandise to sell to your audience:

Know your audience: The first step in selecting merchandise for your podcast is understanding your audience. What are their interests and preferences? What types of products would they be interested in buying? Consider conducting surveys or gathering feedback from your listeners to get a better sense of what they would be interested in purchasing.

Reflect your brand: Your merchandise should reflect the overall brand of your podcast. Consider incorporating your podcast logo or catchphrase into your merchandise designs. This will help to create a sense of cohesiveness between your podcast and your merchandise, making it easier for your audience to connect with and recognize your brand.

Offer unique items: To make your merchandise stand out from the competition, consider offering unique or custom items that can't be found elsewhere. This could include exclusive designs or limited edition products that are only available for a short period of time.

Consider quality and price: When selecting merchandise to sell, it's important to strike a balance between quality and price. You want to offer high-quality products that your audience will be satisfied with, but also at a price point that is affordable and accessible for your listeners.

Leverage your platform: Use your podcast and social media platforms to promote and market your merchandise. Consider offering special promotions or discounts to your listeners to encourage them to make a purchase. You can also showcase your merchandise in your podcast episodes or on your website to increase visibility and awareness.

By using these strategies, you can identify and select the right merchandise to sell to your audience, increasing revenue and building a deeper connection with your listeners.

Tips for promoting your merchandise and encouraging your listeners to make purchases

Creating and selling merchandise related to your podcast can be a great way to generate revenue and connect with your audience. However, with so many products and options available, it can be challenging to decide on the right merchandise to offer.

Here are some strategies for identifying and selecting the right merchandise to sell to your audience:

Know your audience: The first step in selecting merchandise for your podcast is understanding your audience. What are their interests and preferences? What types of products would they be interested in buying? Consider conducting surveys or gathering feedback from your listeners to get a better sense of what they would be interested in purchasing.

Reflect your brand: Your merchandise should reflect the overall brand of your podcast. Consider incorporating your podcast logo or catchphrase into your merchandise designs. This will help to create a sense of cohesiveness between your podcast and your merchandise, making it easier for your audience to connect with and recognize your brand.

Offer unique items: To make your merchandise stand out from the competition, consider offering unique or custom items that can't be found elsewhere. This could include exclusive designs or limited edition products that are only available for a short period of time.

Consider quality and price: When selecting merchandise to sell, it's important to strike a balance between quality and price. You want to offer high-quality products that your audience will be satisfied with, but also at a price point that is affordable and accessible for your listeners.

Leverage your platform: Use your podcast and social media platforms to promote and market your merchandise. Consider offering special promotions or discounts to your listeners to encourage them to make a purchase. You can also showcase your merchandise in your podcast episodes or on your website to increase visibility and awareness.

By using these strategies, you can identify and select the right merchandise to sell to your audience, increasing revenue and building a deeper connection with your listeners.

Best practices for managing your merchandise sales and fulfillment process

Creating and selling merchandise related to your podcast can be a great way to engage with your listeners and generate revenue for your show. However, managing your merchandise sales and fulfillment process can be a complex and time-consuming task. In this chapter, we'll cover some best practices for managing your merchandise sales to ensure that your listeners receive their orders in a timely and efficient manner.

Choose a reliable merchandise partner: When it comes to selling merchandise, it's important to work with a partner that you can trust. Look for a partner with a good reputation, reliable fulfillment processes, and excellent customer service. You should also consider the types of merchandise that they offer, their pricing, and their ability to handle large volumes of orders.

Set clear expectations for processing and shipping times: One of the most important aspects of managing merchandise sales is setting clear expectations for processing and shipping times. Make sure that your listeners know how long it will take for their orders to be processed and shipped, and provide regular updates on the status of their orders. This will help to manage their expectations and reduce the number of inquiries and complaints you receive.

Provide excellent customer service: As with any business, providing excellent customer service is crucial to the success of your merchandise sales. Make sure that your listeners have a way to contact you if they have any questions or concerns about their orders. Respond promptly and professionally to any inquiries or complaints that you receive, and do your best to resolve any issues in a timely and satisfactory manner.

Use quality materials and suppliers: The quality of your merchandise is an important factor in the overall customer experience. Make sure that you use high-quality materials and suppliers to ensure that your merchandise is durable and long-lasting. This will help to build trust with your listeners and encourage them to make future purchases.

Keep accurate records and track inventory: To effectively manage your merchandise sales, it's important to keep accurate records and track your inventory. Use a system to keep track of the orders that you receive, the merchandise that you have in stock, and the items that have been shipped. This will help you to stay organized and ensure that you can fulfill orders in a timely and efficient manner.

Offer refunds and returns: Sometimes, customers may be unhappy with their purchases and may want to return or exchange their merchandise. It's important to have a clear and fair policy for refunds and returns to ensure that your listeners are satisfied with their purchases. Make sure that you clearly communicate your policy to your customers, and be responsive and accommodating to any requests for refunds or exchanges.

Continuously review and improve your processes: As your podcast and merchandise sales grow, it's important to continuously review and improve your processes to ensure that you can meet the needs of your listeners. Pay attention to customer feedback and make changes to your processes as needed. This will help you to provide the best possible experience for your listeners and ensure the success of your merchandise sales.

By following these best practices for managing your merchandise sales and fulfillment process, you can ensure that your listeners receive high-quality merchandise and an excellent customer experience. This will help to build trust and loyalty among your audience, as well as generate revenue for your show.

Conclusion:

Creating and selling merchandise related to your podcast can be a rewarding and profitable venture. By identifying the right products, promoting them to your audience, and efficiently managing your sales and fulfillment process, you can build a successful merchandise business that not only generates revenue but also strengthens the connection between you and your listeners. With the right approach and a bit of creativity, you can turn your podcast into a thriving brand that people are proud to support.

CHAPTER 28: BUILDING A PERSONAL BRAND

❖ Why building a personal brand is important for podcasters
❖ Strategies for defining and building your personal brand around your podcast
❖ Best practices for managing your personal brand across multiple platforms and channels

In today's digital age, building a personal brand is essential for anyone looking to create a successful career in any field. For podcasters, developing a strong personal brand can be the key to standing out in a crowded market and building a loyal fan base. Your personal brand is the unique combination of your skills, personality, values, and experiences that set you apart from others. It is what makes your podcast special and what draws listeners in to become part of your community. In this chapter, we will explore the importance of building a personal brand for podcasters and provide strategies and best practices for doing so.

Why building a personal brand is important for podcasters

As a podcaster, building a personal brand can be an essential part of growing your audience, establishing credibility, and standing out in a crowded market. Your personal brand is essentially the image and reputation you create for yourself, based on your unique skills, values, and expertise. Here are some reasons why building a personal brand is important for podcasters:

Establishing credibility: Building a personal brand can help you establish credibility and authority in your field. By sharing your knowledge, insights, and experiences through your podcast and other channels, you can position yourself as an expert in your niche, which can help you build trust with your audience.

Building a loyal fanbase: A strong personal brand can help you build a loyal fanbase, as listeners become invested in your story and your unique perspective. By sharing your personal experiences, interests, and values, you can connect with your audience on a deeper level, and foster a sense of community and belonging.

Attracting sponsorships and partnerships: When you have a strong personal brand, you can attract potential sponsors and partners who are aligned with your values and message. Sponsors are often looking for influencers who have a dedicated following, and who can help them reach a specific audience.

Differentiating yourself from the competition: With so many podcasts out there, building a personal brand can help you differentiate yourself from the competition. By developing a unique voice and style, and by building a community around your podcast, you can create a strong identity that sets you apart from others in your niche.

Overall, building a personal brand can be a powerful way to grow your podcast, attract new listeners, and establish yourself as an authority in your field.

In the next few chapters, we'll explore some strategies for building your personal brand as a podcaster, including developing your unique voice and style, creating a consistent online presence, and leveraging social media to build your audience.

Strategies for defining and building your personal brand around your podcast

As a podcaster, your personal brand is an extension of your podcast. It's a reflection of your values, your expertise, and your unique perspective. A strong personal brand can help you establish authority in your niche, grow your audience, and attract new opportunities. Here are some strategies for defining and building your personal brand around your podcast:

Define your unique value proposition: What sets you and your podcast apart from others in your niche? What unique perspectives or insights do you bring to the table? Defining your unique value proposition can help you stand out and position yourself as a thought leader in your field.

Establish a consistent visual identity: Your personal brand should have a consistent visual identity across all platforms. This includes your podcast artwork, social media graphics, and website design. Consistency in design helps build recognition and makes your brand more memorable.

Craft a strong personal bio: Your personal bio should communicate your expertise, your passion for your niche, and your unique voice. Use this opportunity to connect with your audience on a personal level and share your story.

Leverage your expertise: As a podcaster, you have a wealth of knowledge in your niche. Use this expertise to build your personal brand by sharing insights and tips on social media, guest posting on relevant blogs, and speaking at events in your field.

Engage with your audience: Building a personal brand is about building relationships with your audience. Engage with your listeners on social media, respond to comments and questions, and seek out opportunities to connect with your community.

Collaborate with other thought leaders in your niche: Collaborating with other thought leaders in your field can help you expand your reach and build your personal brand. Consider partnering with other podcasters, guest posting on each other's blogs, or co-creating content to share with your audiences.

Be authentic: Ultimately, your personal brand is a reflection of who you are. Be true to yourself, and let your personality and values shine through in everything you do.

By following these strategies, you can build a strong personal brand that enhances your podcast and helps you achieve your goals as a podcaster.

Best practices for managing your personal brand across multiple platforms and channels

Once you've established your personal brand as a podcaster, it's important to manage it consistently across all channels and platforms where you have a presence. Here are some best practices for managing your personal brand effectively:

Develop a consistent voice and tone: Consistency is key when it comes to building a personal brand. Your voice and tone should be consistent across all your podcast episodes and social media platforms. Your followers should know what to expect from you and recognize your content when they see it.

Use consistent branding: Your personal brand should be reflected in all aspects of your podcast, from your podcast artwork to your social media profiles. Make sure your branding is consistent across all channels to help your audience recognize your content more easily.

Engage with your audience: Respond to comments, questions, and feedback from your audience. This will help you build a connection with your listeners and establish a sense of community. Engaging with your audience will also help you better understand their needs and preferences, which can help you create more targeted content.

Monitor your online presence: Keep track of what people are saying about you and your podcast online. You can use tools like Google Alerts, social media monitoring tools, and podcast directories to keep tabs on your online reputation. Respond to negative comments or reviews in a professional manner and use feedback to improve your content.

Create content for different channels: Each social media platform has its own unique audience and format. Create content that is tailored to each platform to maximize engagement. For example, Instagram is great for visual content like photos and videos, while Twitter is more text-based and great for engaging in conversations with your audience.

Be authentic: Authenticity is crucial for building a personal brand. Don't try to be someone you're not, and don't pretend to know everything. Share your experiences and be honest about your strengths and weaknesses. This will help you build trust with your audience and establish a loyal following.

Stay organized: Managing your personal brand across multiple platforms can be overwhelming, so it's important to stay organized. Use a social media management tool to schedule posts and monitor your channels. Create a content calendar to plan your podcast episodes and social media content in advance.

By following these best practices, you can effectively manage your personal brand across multiple channels and platforms, helping you to establish a strong and recognizable brand as a podcaster.

Building a personal brand is crucial for podcasters who want to succeed in today's competitive market. By defining and building your brand, you can create a unique and authentic voice that resonates with your audience and helps you stand out in a crowded field. Through consistent and intentional branding efforts, you can create a loyal following and build a successful career in podcasting. Remember, your personal brand is not just about you, but also about your audience, so it's important to stay true to your values and provide value to your listeners. With the right strategies and best practices, you can build a personal brand that will help you achieve your goals and grow your podcast for years to come.

CHAPTER 29: MANAGING YOUR PODCAST BUSINESS FINANCES

❖ Importance of managing your podcast business finances effectively
❖ Maintaining Your Podcast Business Finances
❖ Tax Tips and Deductions for Podacters

Importance of Managing Your Podcast Business Finances Effectively

If you're running a podcast, you're also running a business. And like any other business, it's important to manage your finances effectively to ensure your podcast's long-term success. In this chapter, we'll discuss the importance of managing your podcast business finances effectively, and provide some tips on how to do it.

Why Manage Your Podcast Business Finances?

There are several reasons why managing your podcast business finances is important. Here are a few of the most important ones:

Budgeting: Without a budget, it's easy to overspend on things like equipment, advertising, and other expenses. By creating a budget and tracking your expenses, you can ensure that you're spending your money wisely.

Tax purposes: If you're making money from your podcast, you'll need to pay taxes on that income. By keeping track of your income and expenses throughout the year, you'll be better prepared when tax season comes around.

Long-term planning: Managing your finances effectively can help you plan for the future. By understanding your revenue and expenses, you can make informed decisions about investing in new equipment, hiring staff, or expanding your podcast to new platforms.

Tips for Managing Your Podcast Business Finances

Here are some tips for managing your podcast business finances effectively:

Create a budget: Start by creating a budget that includes all of your expected income and expenses. Be sure to include things like equipment costs, hosting fees, advertising, and any other expenses you expect to incur.

Track your expenses: Keep track of all of your expenses throughout the year. This will make it easier to file your taxes and will help you understand where your money is going.

Use accounting software: Consider using accounting software like QuickBooks or FreshBooks to help you manage your finances. These tools can help you keep track of your income and expenses, create invoices, and manage your accounts.

Separate your personal and business finances: It's important to keep your personal and business finances separate. This will make it easier to track your expenses and ensure that you're paying taxes on the correct income.

Hire a professional: If you're not comfortable managing your own finances, consider hiring a professional accountant or bookkeeper to help you. They can provide guidance on tax planning, financial reporting, and other important financial matters.

Conclusion

Managing your podcast business finances effectively is critical to the long-term success of your podcast. By creating a budget, tracking your expenses, and using accounting software, you can ensure that you're spending your money wisely and making informed decisions about the future of your podcast. If you're not comfortable managing your own finances, consider hiring a professional to help you. With the right financial management practices in place, you'll be well on your way to building a successful and sustainable podcast business.

One of the most critical components of running a successful podcast is effectively managing your business finances. From bookkeeping to taxes, there are several aspects of financial management that podcasters must consider to ensure their financial success. In this chapter, we'll explore strategies for setting up and maintaining your podcast business finances, including bookkeeping, accounting, and taxes.

Setting Up Your Podcast Business Finances
The first step in managing your podcast business finances is setting up your business structure. This can be a daunting task, but it's essential to establish your business as a separate entity from your personal finances to protect your personal assets in case of any legal or financial issues.

There are a few different business structures to consider, including sole proprietorship, partnership, limited liability company (LLC), and corporation. Each structure has its own unique advantages and disadvantages, so it's important to research and choose the one that best fits your specific needs.

Once you've established your business structure, you'll need to obtain any necessary permits or licenses to operate your podcast business legally. This may include registering your business with your state's secretary of state, obtaining a tax ID number, and registering for any required state or local taxes.

Tax Tips and Deductions for Podacters

Once your business is set up, you'll need to establish effective financial management practices to keep your finances in order. Here are some strategies for maintaining your podcast business finances:

Keep Accurate Records

It's essential to keep accurate records of all your podcast business finances, including income, expenses, and any financial transactions. This can be accomplished using financial management software or by hiring a bookkeeper or accountant to manage your finances.

Separate Your Business and Personal Finances

It's critical to keep your business finances separate from your personal finances to ensure accurate bookkeeping and to avoid legal and tax issues. Open a separate bank account and credit card for your podcast business and use them exclusively for your business expenses.

Monitor Your Cash Flow

Cash flow is the lifeblood of any business, including your podcast. It's essential to monitor your cash flow regularly to ensure you have enough funds to cover your expenses and invest in future growth.

Stay on Top of Your Taxes

As a business owner, you'll be responsible for paying taxes on your podcast's income. It's crucial to stay on top of your tax obligations to avoid any legal or financial issues. Consult with a tax professional to ensure you're meeting all your tax requirements and taking advantage of any tax deductions available to you.

Track Your Expenses

Tracking your expenses is essential for accurate bookkeeping and for claiming any business-related tax deductions. Make sure to keep all receipts and records of your podcast-related expenses, and track them regularly to ensure you're staying within your budget.

As a podcaster, it's important to understand the tax implications of your podcast business and take advantage of any tax deductions you may be eligible for. Here are some tax tips and deductions for podcasters to keep in mind:

Keep accurate records: It's essential to keep accurate records of all your podcast-related expenses, income, and receipts. This includes expenses related to equipment, hosting fees, advertising, and any other business expenses.

Deduct equipment expenses: If you purchase equipment specifically for your podcast, such as microphones, headphones, or a mixer, you may be able to deduct the cost of these items as a business expense.

Deduct hosting and production fees: If you pay for hosting or production services for your podcast, these fees may also be deductible as a business expense.

Deduct advertising expenses: If you advertise your podcast on other platforms or pay for promotions to increase your listenership, these expenses may be deductible as a business expense.

Deduct travel expenses: If you travel for your podcast, such as attending events or interviewing guests, you may be able to deduct your travel expenses, including airfare, hotel accommodations, and meals.

Deduct home office expenses: If you use a dedicated space in your home for your podcast, you may be eligible to deduct a portion of your home expenses, including rent or mortgage payments, utilities, and internet fees.

Consult with a tax professional: It's always a good idea to consult with a tax professional to ensure you're taking advantage of all the tax deductions you're eligible for and that you're meeting all your tax obligations.

By keeping accurate records and taking advantage of these tax deductions, you can minimize your tax liability and maximize your profits as a podcaster.

Conclusion

Managing your podcast business finances can seem daunting, but with the right strategies and tools, you can stay on top of your finances and set your podcast up for long-term financial success. Remember to keep accurate records, separate your business and personal finances, monitor your cash flow, stay on top of your taxes, and track your expenses to ensure your podcast business is financially healthy.

CHAPTER 30: THE FUTURE OF PODCASTING: RECAP, REFLECTION, AND LOOKING AHEAD

❖   Recap of the main topics covered in the book
❖   Key takeaways and actionable tips for podcasters
❖   Final advice for podcasters

Recap of the main topics covered in the book

Congratulations! You've made it to the end of this book on podcasting. Over the course of the past 29 chapters, we've covered a wide range of topics, from creating your podcast concept to growing your audience and monetizing your show. Let's take a moment to recap the main points we've covered:

Defining Your Podcast Concept
In the first few chapters, we discussed the importance of defining your podcast concept and understanding your target audience. We talked about choosing a topic that you're passionate about and that resonates with your listeners. We also looked at different formats and styles of podcasts, including interview-style shows, narrative-driven shows, and solo-host shows.

Equipment and Recording Techniques
In the next section, we dove into the technical side of podcasting, discussing the equipment and software you need to record and edit your show. We also covered recording techniques, including microphone placement and using sound effects and music to enhance your show.

Launching and Growing Your Podcast

Once you've recorded and edited your podcast, it's time to launch and grow your show. In this section, we discussed the importance of creating eye-catching cover art, writing compelling episode titles and descriptions, and promoting your show on social media and other channels.

Building and Engaging Your Audience

Your podcast is only as successful as your audience, so in the next section, we looked at strategies for building and engaging your listeners. We discussed the importance of consistent and frequent posting, creating a sense of community and belonging among your audience, and using your show to drive positive change.

Monetizing Your Podcast

In the final few chapters, we talked about different ways to monetize your podcast, including sponsorships and advertising, Patreon, merchandise sales, and personal branding. We discussed strategies for choosing the right monetization strategy for your audience, creating effective sponsorship pitches and negotiating deals, and managing your podcast business finances.

As you can see, there's a lot that goes into creating and growing a successful podcast. But with the right strategy and a lot of hard work, it's definitely possible. And don't forget, there's always room to experiment and try new things, so feel free to explore the world of podcasting and see where it takes you. Good luck, and happy podcasting!

Key takeaways and actionable tips for podcasters

Congratulations! You've made it to the end of the book, and hopefully you've gained a lot of valuable insights and tips for starting, growing, and monetizing your podcast. To help you remember some of the key takeaways, we've put together a list of actionable tips that you can apply to your podcasting journey.

Know your audience and create content that resonates with them: This is one of the most important things you can do as a podcaster. Know who your target audience is and create content that speaks directly to them. This will help you build a loyal following and grow your audience over time.

Invest in quality equipment and sound editing software: While it's possible to start a podcast with just a smartphone, investing in quality equipment and sound editing software can take your podcast to the next level. Your listeners will appreciate the improved sound quality, and you'll be able to create more engaging and professional-sounding episodes.

Consistency is key: Consistency is important for building a loyal audience. Set a regular publishing schedule and stick to it. Whether it's once a week or once a month, your listeners will appreciate knowing when to expect new episodes.

Engage with your listeners: Your listeners are the lifeblood of your podcast, so it's important to engage with them. Encourage them to leave reviews, respond to comments and messages, and even incorporate listener feedback into your episodes.

Monetize your podcast: There are many ways to monetize your podcast, from sponsorships and advertising to merchandise sales and Patreon campaigns. Choose the monetization strategy that works best for your audience and focus on building a loyal following.

Manage your finances: Managing your podcast business finances effectively is important for long-term success. Set up a system for bookkeeping, accounting, and taxes early on, and consider hiring a professional accountant to help you navigate the complexities of running a business.

Never stop learning: The world of podcasting is constantly evolving, so it's important to stay up-to-date with the latest trends and best practices. Join podcasting communities, attend conferences and webinars, and read industry publications to stay informed and learn from other podcasters.

This list is by no means exhaustive, but it covers some of the most important takeaways and actionable tips for podcasters. Remember, building a successful podcast takes time, effort, and dedication, but with the right strategy and mindset, you can create a podcast that engages and inspires your listeners. Good luck on your podcasting journey, and happy podcasting!

Final advice for podcasters

By now, you should have a good understanding of the key concepts and strategies for creating, launching, and growing a successful podcast. However, before you embark on your podcasting journey, here are some final thoughts and advice to keep in mind:

Be Yourself: Authenticity is key to building a loyal audience. Don't try to be someone you're not or pretend to know more than you do. Be honest and genuine in your podcast, and your audience will appreciate it.

Consistency is Key: Consistency in content, branding, and schedule is crucial for building a reliable audience. Aim for a consistent release schedule, consistent quality of content, and consistent branding to help your audience identify and connect with your show.

Engage with Your Audience: Interacting with your audience can help you better understand their needs and interests, and ultimately make your show more engaging and valuable. Encourage feedback and respond to comments and messages, and create opportunities for your listeners to connect with each other and with you.

Keep Learning and Growing: The world of podcasting is constantly evolving, so stay up to date with the latest trends and best practices. Listen to other podcasts, read industry blogs, and attend conferences to learn from other podcasters and improve your skills.

Enjoy the Journey: Podcasting can be a challenging and time-consuming process, but it can also be a rewarding and fulfilling one. Enjoy the journey, and don't forget to have fun and stay passionate about your content.

In addition to these final thoughts, here are some other tips and advice that didn't fit neatly into the previous chapters:

Embrace Imperfection: Don't wait for everything to be perfect before launching your podcast. There will always be room for improvement, so focus on getting started and improving as you go.

Use Quality Equipment: While you don't need the most expensive equipment, investing in good quality gear can make a huge difference in the sound quality of your podcast.

Be Prepared for Technical Issues: Technical issues can and will happen, so be prepared to troubleshoot and have a backup plan in case of equipment failure or other technical problems.

Experiment and Innovate: Don't be afraid to try new things and experiment with different formats or styles. Podcasting is a creative medium, so take advantage of that and push the boundaries of what's possible.

In conclusion, podcasting can be a challenging but rewarding journey. With the tips and strategies outlined in this book, you're well on your way to creating and growing a successful podcast. Remember to stay true to yourself, be consistent, engage with your audience, keep learning, and above all, have fun! Good luck on your podcasting journey!

Final Thoughts and Advice for Podcasters

Congratulations on making it to the end of this book! By now, you should have a good understanding of the key concepts and strategies for creating, launching, and growing a successful podcast. However, before you embark on your podcasting journey, here are some final thoughts and advice to keep in mind:

Be Yourself: Authenticity is key to building a loyal audience. Don't try to be someone you're not or pretend to know more than you do. Be honest and genuine in your podcast, and your audience will appreciate it.

Consistency is Key: Consistency in content, branding, and schedule is crucial for building a reliable audience. Aim for a consistent release schedule, consistent quality of content, and consistent branding to help your audience identify and connect with your show.

Engage with Your Audience: Interacting with your audience can help you better understand their needs and interests, and ultimately make your show more engaging and valuable. Encourage feedback and respond to comments and messages, and create opportunities for your listeners to connect with each other and with you.

Keep Learning and Growing: The world of podcasting is constantly evolving, so stay up to date with the latest trends and best practices. Listen to other podcasts, read industry blogs, and attend conferences to learn from other podcasters and improve your skills.

Enjoy the Journey: Podcasting can be a challenging and time-consuming process, but it can also be a rewarding and fulfilling one.

Enjoy the journey, and don't forget to have fun and stay passionate about your content.

In addition to these final thoughts, here are some other tips and advice that didn't fit neatly into the previous chapters:

Embrace Imperfection: Don't wait for everything to be perfect before launching your podcast. There will always be room for improvement, so focus on getting started and improving as you go.

Use Quality Equipment: While you don't need the most expensive equipment, investing in good quality gear can make a huge difference in the sound quality of your podcast.

Be Prepared for Technical Issues: Technical issues can and will happen, so be prepared to troubleshoot and have a backup plan in case of equipment failure or other technical problems.

Experiment and Innovate: Don't be afraid to try new things and experiment with different formats or styles. Podcasting is a creative medium, so take advantage of that and push the boundaries of what's possible.

In conclusion, podcasting can be a challenging but rewarding journey. With the tips and strategies outlined in this book, you're well on your way to creating and growing a successful podcast. Remember to stay true to yourself, be consistent, engage with your audience, keep learning, and above all, have fun! Good luck on your podcasting journey!

www.ingramcontent.com/pod-product-compliance
Lightning Source LLC
Chambersburg PA
CBHW040918210326
41597CB00030B/5118